The Healing of the African American Soul

With

Truth and Reconciliation

BY WALI SABIR

Edited by Daoud Shariff

The Healing of the African American Soul
With
Truth and Reconciliation

Copyright ©2021 Sabir Publishing

All rights reserved. No part of this book may be reproduced, stored in a retrieval system, or transmitted in any form or by any means electronic, mechanical, photo copying, recording, or otherwise, without written permission from the publisher.

Wali Sabir
Sabir Publishing
 (214) 370-5612
https://www.projectstandup.net
climatesuccess@gmail.com

ISBN: 979-8-9850321-0-9

THE APPEAL

Our social blood is flowing.

From words, we use without knowing.

Putting labels on humans like black and white,

Weapons of mass destruction causing human blight.

Artificially elevating some in a spell, while others descend to a living hell.

With the force and the power of Government ways,

As they cast their spell, all human life pays.

Know you! The Truth is now at hand.

Real women and men are taking their stand.

Refusing the darkness or be blinded by light.

Not the extreme left nor the extreme right!

With this Declaration of Commitment, we lay out our case.

We can no longer ignore that which stares us in our face.

With Truth! is the only way we will heal!

Truth and Reconciliation is our strongest appeal!

Table of Contents

Acknowledgment 1
About The Author 3
Preface 5
Introduction 7
Chapter 1: How To Know The Truth 20
    Belief 29
    Real Relief 32
    Elevate Your Expectation 34
Chapter 2: Our Soul in Crisis 36
    America's Pathology 62
Chapter 3: Hemorrhaging of Social Intelligence 68
Michael P. Watson 68
    The Elephant in the Room 79
Chapter 4: The Cascade of Healing in Reverse 82
    Frederick Douglass 94
    We got to get it right 95
Chapter 5: The Cascade of Social Healing 98
    Frederick Douglass 112
    Word Environment Exercise 112

Chapter 6: STAND UP 116
    C.C.E.D.G. 125
    PROJECT STAND-UP! 128
    Dear Human Family, ...137
Social Science / Philosophical History 140
Afterword 142

Acknowledgment

I am eternally grateful for all the forerunners, our heroes, and sheroes that made it possible for us to get to this present day, the day of conclusion. The day when everything done in the dark is coming to light.

There is a long list of contributors to this work: family, friends, and others committed to this righteous cause. Their support, encouragement, and faith that the arc of justice would bend to cover us, the formerly enslaved people, has strengthened my faith and determination to keep going.

I am reluctant to start naming people because the list is so long. So, let me point to some sources that I have drawn upon in this work as a means of acknowledgment and gratitude for the contributions they have made and are making.

The volumes of works available in the public space by Imam W. Deen Mohammed and the ongoing editorial and publication of his work and commentary by Imam Ronald Shahid. This work is the seed bed from which many of the ideas in this book have sprouted forth.

Another contributor to this work is Instructor Benjamin Bilal; his classes and publications are a deep well of refreshing insights to light the path of human growth and development.

Also, I have recently come across some scholarly works that I believe is a must-read for factual and statistical substantiation and would like to thank each one of these authors for their contributions:

Shaw Rochester's book "Black Tax", Brian

Introduction

Stevenson's book "Just Mercy," Michelle Alexander's "The New Jim Crow," Robin Diamgelo's book on "White Fragility," Mehrsa Baradaran's book "The Color of Acknowledgment Money", Richard Rothstein's book, "The Color of Law," and last in this short list, but not least in the contribution is Jacqueline Battalora's book "The Birth of The White Nation."

I close the acknowledgments with deep regard and thanks to my dear friends and companions, Abdul Hakim Yamini; your profound wisdom is a source of light. I appreciate your council and encouragement in the unfolding of this work.

Daoud Shariff, your keen intellect and editorial skills is a needed support for my raw and down-to-earth writing style.

And last but not least, thanks to my dear cousin, Diane Riggsbee, your technical support is unmatched. Most of all, I am grateful to The Creator for life, the heart, the mind, and the spirit that He has endowed me with, to forward our ongoing mission to remake this world, starting with our own selves.

Introduction

About The Author

Wali A. Sabir, born to Mr. Mossett and Mrs. Vallie Harris of Durham, North Carolina, on July 29, 1945, was the fifth of nine children. My writing career grew out of my concern for my own family as well as my own heritage as a member of the African American ethnic and cultural group.

As a very young man, while in Junior high school, I became actively involved in the civil rights movement. My involvement gave rise to some intense thoughts about the meaning of civil rights and human rights and how my people in America could achieve those rights.

My thoughts caused me to ask many questions that could not be answered by the common leaders nor the average participants in the civil rights movement. The quest for answers led me to solutions that I only found in the Nation of Islam. I was motivated by the teachings, and I joined the Nation of Islam Movement in October of 1971.

As a devoted follower of the Honorable Elijah Muhammad (the prayers and peace be upon him), I served as an assistant minister, a minister, a teacher, and Dean of boys of the University of Islam in Raleigh Durham, North Carolina. I soon came to be responsible for various other duties. There was a need for many services, which required me to wear multiple hats. My sense of responsibility compelled me to wear designations from time to time, ranging from baker to builder to community minister.

Introduction

When the leadership transition came in 1975, I greeted it wholeheartedly, with open arms, mind, heart, and spirit.

As a devoted, informed, and conscious follower of the directives of the Honorable Elijah Muhammad, I then became a dedicated follower of the Honorable Imam W. Deen Mohammed and his direction, widely designated as America's Imam and foremost international Muslim American leader. I was inspired to develop my writing talents in pursuit of meeting the unique cultural needs of my own beloved family in particular and the African American community in general.

Imam Mohammed once stated profoundly that "life has no meaning without definition." True definition provides true direction. My lifework strives to shed light on the definitions of important internal and external factors instilled into our society that helped to form and shape our lives. It is providential work such as "life's definitions" that sets the stage through a language cultural medium for us to consciously seize self-control and give greater importance, meaning, and enhancement to our own lives and life direction.

I have shared my thoughts and perceptions by publishing three other books aimed to inform for self-reflection and community reading pleasure; the first is titled: "The Reconstruction of the African American Male" in 1989. Second, "The Anatomy of Change" in 2013. And third, Liberating Minds From Oppressive Word Environments" in 2017. There is an order and a continuity in these publications, which I encourage you to order, read and retain as a reference in your library. Daoud Shariff was also my editor in the last two of my previous publications.

Introduction

Preface

With The Name Of our Creator, Guardian, Evolver, and Sustainer, Who Is to His creation, The Most Gracious and The Most Merciful.

My dear respected brother, my companion in our lifework, asked me to pen a preface for his newest book. In gathering my thoughts about what to say in what I see and believe to be one of the most serious issues of our time, I had to ask myself the purpose of the preface? Beyond that, I had to reflect on some of the deeper meanings that could drive home the timeliness of this title, "The Healing of the African American Soul with Truth and Reconciliation."

The general understanding of the preface is to introduce the book's title, subject, and aim. Digging a little deeper than the general understanding, I thought about the fact that "preface" is made up of two components, "pre," which means before, and "face," which points to character. It has been said that the "Face" of a thing is the first sign of the nature of a thing.

By studying the face of a thing, you can, over time, get a firm picture in your mind of the natural disposition or character of that particular thing. In this case, we are not only talking about the character of a person, but we are also talking about the character of a natural movement simultaneously.

Over the last forty-five years, I have had the pleasure of working side by side with Wali Abdul Sabir in the ongoing mission of remaking the world and reclaiming as many of our people that would hear and take heed to the call. To come alive to the opportunity to take charge of our present and our future lives as human beings. Through this

Introduction

work, I have learned something about his character and the movement he is committed to through his life work. During this time, I had the opportunity to meet and be in the company of his loving family and be in the presence of some powerful family roots. I accepted his mother as if she was my own mother. A powerful and precious family tree that still produces leaders grounded in human excellence for our community service and development, even today.

I can say without hesitation that my brother Wali Abdul Sabir has shown me through his work that he has remained faithful to his calling to be an engineer, builder, and thinker in the movement. That is remaking the world, even as we speak. Wali's work has focused on the "dynamic movement of words" as in the body of language systems from his very first book to his most recent work.

Words in their intrinsic meaning have shaped global citizens' character in powerful ways that the people themselves most often are entirely oblivious to.

In his work, he points out the difference between words as they organically evolve into natural language systems giving rise to a genuinely human character on the one hand. And on the other hand, words rooted in corrupt intent give rise to language systems like that we have actively alive in the global community today.

Today, without question, we have a planned-demic of hate, negativity, and inhuman behavior. Today, without question, people are becoming more entrenched in their extreme and polarized views with no conscious concept of the universality of truth that they relate to. Therefore, in this pre-face, I feel compelled to point out the need for nature-based work to be consciously imbibed before we can change the character of the prevailing culture today.

Introduction

The Healing of the African American Soul with Truth and Reconciliation

"If you hear the dogs, keep going. If you see the torches in the woods, keep going. If there's shouting after you, keep going. Don't ever stop. Keep going. If you want a taste of freedom, keep going."

Harriet Tubman

When I was a boy, everything seemed larger than life; my town was big, my state was huge, and I still had no concept of the vastness of the earth. Not only did the world seem more significant than I could conceive, but time itself seemed as though, in and of itself, moved slowly across the vastness of space. The days seemed long, and months and years seemed to take forever. Traveling long distances was limited because of time constraints.

Likewise, news also traveled very slowly, and people were isolated in their little pockets, unaware of what was going on in other distant and some nearer places. We knew extraordinarily little about other people and social events other than the ones taking place relatively close to us. Whatever was written in print was considered the law, no matter who wrote it or their motivation for writing it.

In every society, the masses of the people have always been less informed than the small group of leaders at the top of the societal pyramid. Moreover, the masses are

Introduction

usually the least prepared to meet the unfolding challenges of an unpredictable social life. Throughout history, the small group of ruling elites have always used time and the crawling speed of information dissemination to their own advantage, in order primarily to keep the masses uninformed, subjugated, vulnerable, manipulatable, and powerless.

Historically, the ruling elite has taken this position simply because they believe in the masses, the grassroots people, or the people they referred to as the common folk. Their view toward the masses, the common people, has been consistent. And that view is that the life of an ordinary person is of less value than their own. Moreover, that the common people only exist to serve their own plans. "I" am better than "you!"

They see the masses like they see livestock, to be used as a food source at the bottom of their economic food chain and to be used for consumption to increase their wealth and personal bottom-line. When they had a total monopoly on the distribution of information, they ensured that the only information that got out to the ordinary people was the information that was manipulatable and delivered as an advantage to themselves, the self-serving elite.

Every society has social systems that are designed to address specific fundamental needs of the people. These systems cover the need of the people to be informed of certain information needed for social functionality, conveyed to the people through the institution of 1) Education (science) and harnessing the forces of habit. The need for earning a living and managing financial resources is addressed through the institutional focus of 2) Economics (and business commerce). The necessity of

Introduction

people to adhere to a social contract for honoring morals, values, heritage, and principal traditions structured to preserve order, direction, and guidance in the life of the people and is passed on from one generation to the next, is atmospherically encompassed in the 3) Cultural (philosophical) life of the people. The need for people to live within and abide by established rules and regulations to manage their affairs based upon agreed social standards, principles, and laws are addressed through the institution of 4) Government (politics).

Stated simply, The Creator has given us basic patterns of fours that range from the nonmaterial to the material manifestations of life. However, the ultimate expression of material life is back to an ever-evolving state of spirituality. The human being is a social creature by nature, which is another way of saying that they are spiritual by nature. It is a well-established fact The Creator uses the concrete form in creation to reveal to us the higher principles of the non-concrete nature of His creation. We must see these social institutions as embodiments of principles necessary to advance human civilization in a balanced way.

Being fully aware of these social institutions and how they should function to serve the general public's best interest, the ruling elite effectively uses their control and influence over these institutions. Their objective is only to distribute inadequate information to ensure that the public is restricted and gets limited access to the total truth and about liberating information needed by the public to clearly understand what is in the public's own best interest.

As an example, education has been used by the industrialist, who fund it, to promote the training of

Introduction

workers to meet their needs in production but more cynical is also their comprehensive plot to create indiscriminate consumers.

Where the exploitative perception of need indeed drove supply and demand, the masses were sold on an impressionable idea. An idea that was converted to supply and demand and hinged upon wants and manipulated desires that perceptively elevated one's social status. The limited exposure to truly, beneficial information impacts how we address meeting all of our natural societal needs. With poor and incomplete information, we tend to make poor and deficient decisions. These poor decisions are often rooted in, directed by, or connected to the ruling class's low expectations of the masses. These low expectations are instilled in them and are in conjunction with the low expectations that the masses of people are now conditioned to have for themselves.

Today, we live in a different world. The old information monopolies and silos are all but dying. Technology has made the vast world seem very small; the slow movement of time is now lightning fast. And information and travel has been reduced to jet time, present time, global real-time with the enhancing advent of the internet. Anything questionable can be fact-checked in seconds.

Lies, falsehoods, and mistruths that have stood supported and unchallenged for centuries are now dispelled within seconds. People are consciously rising up all over the globe to fight tyranny and oppression. The blockchain and decentralized cryptocurrency were developed to protest corrupted governments and corrupt

Introduction

business practices everywhere. Modern science technology is at work, automatically helping to level the playing field.

Yes! We live in a unique time that is unprecedented in the history of the human journey on this planet. It is a prophetic time that we have already been forewarned about. A time when everything hidden would come to light. There is no greater example of that happening than right now. In this time, it is being publicly revealed, even to the common people, how there has been a deliberate and concerted affront on all aspects of life of the formally enslaved people in America and their descendants. This affront is designed and orchestrated to ensure that we, the ex-slaves, would be deprived of every joint effort, every consideration afforded to all other American people to ensure that other Americans successfully establish themselves in the land.

It has come to light how the U.S. Government cold-heartedly and calculatingly created the ghetto, with its planned abject poverty, demarcation, deprivation, and consequential socio-economic dysfunctions. While at the same time, the U.S. Government was channeling its vast resources to build and populate the affluent suburbs. It is clear that the ghetto, poverty, bad health, the prison industrial complex, broken families, and so on are the planned destiny for the formally enslaved people. Intentionally, this was done at the hands of those controlling our narrative, the levers of power, and the effective instruments of social engineering.

Why has our government, in its covert agenda, not allowed its African Descendants of Slavery, specifically the Constitutional right to life, freedom, liberty, and the pursuit of happiness promised to all Americans?

Introduction

Consider the following scripture from the Quran:

(47:29) Or do they, in whose hearts there is a sickness, believe that The Creator will not bring their failings to light?

(47:30) If We were to so will, We could have shown them to you so that you would recognize them by their faces, and you would certainly know them by the manner of their speech. The Creator knows all your deeds.

(47:31) We shall certainly test you until We know those of you who truly strive and remain steadfast, and will ascertain about you.

(47:32) Those who disbelieved and barred others from the way of The Creator and opposed the Messenger after the True Guidance had become manifest to them, they shall not be able to cause The Creator the least harm; rather, He will reduce all their works to nought.[39]

(47:33) Believers, obey The Creator and obey the Messenger and do not cause your works to be nullified.[40]

(47:34) Verily, The Creator shall not forgive those who disbelieved and barred others from His Way and clung to their unbelief until their death.

(47:35) So, be not faint-hearted and do not cry for peace.[41] You shall prevail. The Creator is with you and will not bring your works to naught.

(47:36) The life of this world is but sport and amusement.[42] If you believe and are G-d-fearing, He will grant you your reward, and will not ask you for your possessions.[43]

(47:37) If He were to ask you for your possessions and press you (in that regard), you would have grown stingy and The Creator would have brought your failings to light.[44]

(47:38) Behold, you are those who are called upon to spend in The Creator's Way, but some of you are stingy.

Introduction

Whoever is stingy is in fact stingy to himself. For The Creator is All-Sufficient, whereas it is you who are in need of Him. If you turn away, He will replace you by a people other than you, and they will not be like you.

It should be noted that it has never been made more explicit than it is today that our social situational dilemma is the result of a designed, carefully orchestrated, and highly qualified plan. In this American Experiment, the social engineering manipulators who formulated and constructed the environment for our social existence left nothing regarding our future destiny to chance. They clearly understood the natural constitution of actual human makeup and aspirations in its most delicate developmental details. They knew that physical containment was only partially effective and could only last for so long. They clearly understood that mental and spiritual containment was the more definitive, decisive, and most effective path they must go down to make a long-lasting, genuinely successful dependent slave.

Understanding that the human being is a spiritual creature with a material form to express the fullness of his human and spiritual potential, they realized they had to reverse the human development process. They developed a counter plan to make the spiritual secondary and subservient to the material. They understood that words make people, and just like words make people, the correct formulation and combination of words can also *unmake* people. The tendency seems to reverse the natural order, turn everything upside down and flip the natural script.

The architects of this plan, which I call social engineering manipulators, understood that they were

Introduction

warring with a strong, spiritually based people. They aimed to capture and control our spirit. They also understood that the people they had declared war upon had the moral high ground, and the only chance that their plan could succeed would also be to corrupt them and unseat them from their morally high, consequential position.

The social engineering manipulators devised an in-depth, very sophisticated language environment, loaded with words that were like explosive land mines and all kinds of potent, highly charged word definitions designed to be used as weapons of mass social destruction. This language was materialized and fertilized with igniters planted in terms of black and white and applied to be instilled in the culture of the people. The very idea of The Creator was even personified and embodied in the term white and pure. At the same time, the concept of the devil, evil, and destruction was represented opposingly in the term black.

To make their game plan work, they had to put all the elements of societal life that they understood into play sociologically and into context. A detailed script was written for the four societal institutions: education, economics, government, and culture, along with the specific language body that they must be based in and operate from. Most important of all, to ensure effective mass devastation, their plan had to carry the weight and force of official high-level and local-level government policy behind it, and it did.

Therefore, we, descendants of the formerly enslaved people, must first and foremost reclaim our rightful position on the moral high ground. The low-frequency

Introduction

words of the slave culture unconsciously oppress us and have taken us down from the moral high ground that Frederick Douglass and Harriet Tubman, et al., stood upon and yearned for. The most glaring example of how far the language of slave culture is woven is our inability to unite around our everyday needs and aspirations.

Most of us indeed want the same thing. We want peace of mind, safety, and security for our families and community. We want to fulfill our unique purpose for our own creation through life, liberty, and the pursuit of happiness. However, something pervading in the language environment prevents the formerly enslaved people from uniting and organizing for our common cause and mutual benefit.

It is reported that the Last and Final Prophet said, and I paraphrase: we won't have success until we believe, and we won't believe until we love for our fellow human being, that which we love for our own self. I contend that the language of slave culture, black and white, makes it impossible for us to truly, love one another. In fact, it is a language that, by design, will not even allow us to love ourselves definitively.

The nature of the language subconsciously creates self-rejection, distrust, and undue suspicion, and an environment that cannot socially support mutual trust and cooperation. For us, as an oppressed people, this is deadly and fatal. We, ourselves, are the most significant resource that we have. And the social engineering manipulators did everything imaginable in their power to devise self-hatred, to make sure that we would not be able to tap into that internal source of power, unity, and enduring strength.

Introduction

The natural world, as established by our Creator, is built on truth. Truth is absolute, meaning the principles that make up truth are consistent; they do not change. People are dynamic; they constantly change in space and through time. Yet, the principles of truth are pliable. They are applicable according to prevailing conditions while retaining the true principle. This principle can be seen in the movement of developmental life from weakness to strength or from immaturity to maturity.

The message in this book is a call for truth and reconciliation. This is the only sustainable and long-lasting salvation for our country. America has survived because of its promise. It advocates a dream. It promises freedom, justice, and equality. The judgment is at hand; The Creator Has Ordered Justice, and the ex-slaves had to be socially prepared over time to receive proper justice.

That time has come. We were not ready previously, perhaps, in our unaware, immature, and unconscious states of redevelopment. Now, we are equipped to not only reconstruct ourselves but we are also equipped to reconstruct our world. And further, equipped to remake the whole world. Words make people, and we are standing here and now, on and in the words of the One That Created us. We have been prepared to STAND UP! as true human beings.

Introduction
Social justice, not socialism

Is it socialism to want the rich to bear their fair share?
Is it socialism to want all to have access to decent health care?
Is it socialism to want to level the playing field?
Is it socialism to want the little guy to get a fair and just deal?
Is its physical responsibility as you claim?
Or is it bigotry by another name?
If we are to live in this world as human beings, We must be council not to be given to any extremes!
Not going to the extreme on the right or left,
Holier than thou, claiming G-d's goodness only for self!
Nor should we be so carefree,
That our lives carry no responsibility!
So, I ask you again.
To think before you sin!
Is it socialism to want the rich to bare – their just and fair share?
Is it socialism to want good health care for all?
Not just the big but equally the small!
Is it socialism when 1% that own 95% of the country's wealth?
Are asked to be good stewards for the good of the country's health?
Is its physical responsibility as you claim?
Or is it bigotry by another name?
Toward faith and good deeds, we all should relate!
With social justice as our moral mandate!
We were created and given the best form!
Toward uprightness and balance as our norm!

Introduction

With a solid moral foundation and deep spiritual insight, Social justice must be our shield and beckoning light!
Wanting for others what we want for self!
Putting our faith in action, not on the shelf!
Pulling back the cover of bigotry and all its schism!
Standing for social justice not socialism!
Without fail we must live what we believe!
Our true self nor G-d can we deceive! We have been given dominion to be fruitful and to multiply!
From dust to industry must be the mantra we live by!
Lest we commit an unforgivable sin!
Let me ask this question again?
Is it socialism to want the rich to carry their fair share?
Is it socialism to want all to have access to decent health care?
Is it socialism to want to level the playing field?
Is it socialism to want the little guy to get a fair and just deal?
Is its physical responsibility as you claim,
or is it bigotry by another name?
Do you play by the rules you as others to go by?
Puling the rug from the public's feet, while pointing to the sky?
You claim G-d, family and country are your priority,
You swear by your life to stand and defend our liberty,
But you close your eyes to your brother's greed,
You change the books to cover up his lawless deed!
What ism drives your philosophy?
Is it the "just for us" democracy?
Why are you so quick to brand and label?

Introduction

Is it that you don't want truth at the round table?
Is its physical responsibility as you claim?
Or is it bigotry by another name?
Let's pray that G-d bless our individual and collective soul,
To come into our special and unique human role!
The path to be truly free!
Is told in our collective history!
Our human chain is no stronger than our weakest link!
We fight for the dignity of the least of us, lest we all sink!
G-d was in the design of this great land.
All control is in the grasp of His Almighty Hand!
In G-d plan there is never scarcity!
You reap what you sow is His law or reciprocity.
We should never pray that another human being fails.
Being true to our human self we will excel!
No other part of the human puzzle can fit your unique space.
So set your sail and get in the human race!
Run against your own mediocrity or bigotry!
Run against any form of human slavery!
So, ask yourself what thoughts drives your philosophy?
Is its physical responsibility as you claim?
Or is it bigotry by another name?

Wali Sabir
9/20/2011

Chapter 1: How To Know The Truth

"Twant me, 'twas The Lord. I always Told Him, 'I Trust To You. I don't know where to go or what to do, but I expect You To Lead me,' and He Always Did."

Harriet Tubman

"Say what you have to say, not what you ought. Any truth is better than make-believe."

Henry David Thoreau

We are now living in the Information Age. Even at a time like this, we also have a deviation from the truth, alternative facts, fake news, ruses, tricks, swindles, hoodwinks, hoaxes, and political spins to sway people in one way or another, for whatever reason. In such an environment, it is understandable that a good number of the public do not even know just what to believe. Even more severe than that, many find it difficult to clearly discern truth from falsehood because of their lack of proper foundational knowledge.

The saying that these are times that trouble men's souls could not be more accurate. Such times suggest that many people do not know what truth is; and how to distinguish truth from non-truth and falsehood. It stands to reason that we must refer to The Author of the truth to know the truth. Who Is the Author of truth? None other than The Creator of us all, The Only True Reality. The Originator of all truth.

The Healing of the African American Soul

John 8:32: ***And ye shall know the truth, and the truth shall set you free.***

Quran 22:6 states: ***That is because The Creator Is The Truth and because He gives life to the dead and because He Is over all things competent.***

The Originator of creation, States That He Created everything in truth, not in falsehood; it then stands to reason, to know truth, we must be students of that which was created in truth, The Creator's creation that is everywhere around and inside of us.

At the center of our eye, there is a part called the iris; in the center of the iris, there is a circle called the pupil. The pupil allows light to strike the retina. The **retina** is a thin layer of tissue that lines the back of the eye on the inside. It is located in front of the optic nerve. The purpose of the **retina** is to receive light that the lens has focused upon, convert the light into neural signals and send these signals on to the brain for visual recognition.

Definitively, the pupil is also another name for a student. The images that we see through the pupil are things that The Creator has created. Therefore, our first teacher is the Creator. **So, the more we study creation, the more we come to know about truth.**

As students of creation, we should bring our attention to the **nature** of creation. We must bring it all together in a unification. Here we are referring to universal laws or patterns on which everything in creation is based. To understand these laws or customs, we must not confuse them with values like good and evil or wrong and right. Universal laws transcend the qualification of good and evil. Such quantifiable values, like good and bad, are relative

The Healing of the African American Soul

and not universal principles in all situations. What is good or right in one case may be bad or wrong in another.

As natural students, we have been endowed with tools to work with; the most important tools we have are our senses. Reality is described primarily as the world or the state of things as we perceive them to actually and conceivably exist; "what is." How do we know what is? The only way we can know the state of things as they actually exist or what it is through the windows of our endowed senses.

It is through the window of our senses that were bestowed upon us that the human being observed the natural patterns of creation and thereby codified them and structured them into laws and principles to abide by. Most notably is the fact that we have the mother book of nature and creation itself to verify the integrity of these laws. What distinguishes the human being as the highest form of creation is their cognitive abilities, particularly the ability to think.

There can be no accurate reasoning or thinking without proper sense perception. Therefore, our ability as human beings to live and socialize in truth and enlightenment depends upon accurate sense perception. Accurate sense perception is a dynamic process that keeps us present and connected to the status of each of our fleeting moments in conjunction with our memory, where decisions are made for proper adaptation to our current environmental condition in a relative state of balance and forward movement.

When our environment gives us information, it usually comes to us in the form of language, in one form or another. That language is processed based on information

The Healing of the African American Soul

that has already been stored in the mental makeup of the mind. We must first determine whether this is something we know about, have some vague knowledge of, or do not know about, at all. To the degree that we can line this information up from memory within ourselves, with the natural patterns we can relate to in the outer creation, we come to know if it can be trusted as accurate. To the degree that it goes counter to the natural patterns in creation, we must reject it as falsehood. To the degree that we are unsure, our common sense tells us to get and ascertain more information.

Truth itself is a healing force. Healing suggests a process to restore health. Health is described as a state of complete emotional and physical well-being. Homeostasis. Balance. A natural state of equilibrium. Physically, Emotionally, Intellectually, Spiritually, and all effective Socially. If truth is healing, its opposite is a disease, dis-ease, falsehood, and lies.

Life in its optimal state is whole, balanced, and healthy, free of sickness and dis-ease. Yet, we live in a society and in a world where there are many sicknesses and diseases. While most of the attention is paid to address the physical illness, very little attention is geared to address the underlying causes and roots of the sickness: falsehoods, weak ideas, and corrupted, wrong thinking.

In fact, the treatment of sickness and disease is one of the largest industries worldwide. We live in a diseased world. There is a lot of money being made on people being sick and keeping people sick; profit results because no one wants to be sick and no one wants to have any disease. Truth-telling must be unapologetically restored and

The Healing of the African American Soul broadly applied worldwide to restore health in a world with such sicknesses.

Even though surely, none of us wants to be sick or wrong, one would be hard-pressed to find any individual or any family that models a state of complete emotional and physical well-being. I have asked this question many times before, who do you know that wants to be wrong? I have not met anyone that wanted to be wrong. Aside from some of us wanting and hoping to be wrong about being right, regarding things that we prefer not to be or not to see.

One could even ask, who do you know that wants to be sick? If everyone in their right nature wants to be right and well, then what is the problem? The problem is misinformation, lies, weak ideas, and corrupted thinking. Lying is big business, as we previously stated. Lying is now an art firmly rooted in the cultural, economic, educational, and governmental life of the society.

Lying and deception are so prevalent and pretty much expected because it has been embedded and strategically built into the cultural fabric using the prevailing tool we use to think and communicate with <u>our language</u>. Language is comprehensively described as "*a whole body of uttered signs employed and understood by a given community as expressions of its thoughts; the aggregate of words, and of methods of their combination into sentences, used in a community for communication and recording and for carrying on the processes of thought.*"

Language is a socially developed medium of expressing thoughts, ideas, concepts, and conveying understanding. It stands to reason that in a world with so much sickness and disease, the words that make up the language systems of communication are logically encoded

The Healing of the African American Soul

with disease and sickness. Therefore our aim must be to understand what constitutes health and well-being?

We know that the health and well-being of our physical bodies is primarily determined by the physical food we eat. We are what we eat! More importantly, we, the nonphysical human being, are also the words that we eat. The principle doesn't change. Inferred to by the phrase "Readers Digest." In our culture, the words we eat are staged in a "spell." As a child, the first thing we are taught is spelling. *The term 'spell' is generally used for magical procedures which cause harm or force people to do something against their will.*

In a world of haves and have – nots and winners and losers, in most cases, the former has worked to spellbind the latter. The few at the top of the social order have always viewed the masses as vulgar, as this word was used to describe the common people in the Latin language. Vulgar is also described as lacking sophistication or good taste; unrefined; uncultured. This view of the few toward the many allowed the few to establish a social framework where the many would be deprived of their G-d given rights to cultivate and pursue their unique gifts and talents and make profound contributions as their own sociological investments toward the common good of the community as a whole.

Such a social framework to function in is very restrictive and repressive. The few, having cast the views and expectations of the many, accordingly, frame them socially, within a state of low human worth and limited value. This is an excellent challenge for all humanity. We have been subjected and conditioned by social manipulators into a system that even renders us to have

The Healing of the African American Soul

such low estimation of our own value and worth as human beings and minimal expectation of our own selves.

Throughout history, the ruling elite has managed and manipulated this process for their own economic benefit. The most practical, powerful utility and tool they have had at their disposal and command is linguistic information. Not just general knowledge in terms of making people aware of the happenings in their environment.

More importantly, information as it is processed through oppressive language. The lens of language determines how we see ourselves and perceive and decode words that describe the relationship with the rest of creation and of one thing in connection with another. In such an unnatural everyday environment, principles like honesty, humility, sincerity, and patience are not the rule in social interaction and social situations; they are often the exception.

Dr. Jacqueline Battalora, J.D., in her book "Birth of the White Nation," tells the story of when, where, and how European people became (so-called) "white." She reveals from her research that whiteness was a notion of the British that was initially synonymous with Christianity. People in colonial life of the early 1600s commonly referred to themselves and others based on their place of origin. There were just two classes of people in colonial society: the elite and the poor masses, the lords and the common folk.

Her research shows that people among the masses, the common people, regardless of where they were from, saw themselves as equals. If they were free persons, they had equal rights and opportunities under the law. If they were indentured servants or in slavitude, they all were treated the same as anyone else with that same social

The Healing of the African American Soul

status. Because of the masses of people, the so-called common lot, the fact that they shared the same poverty eventually led to the Bakers Rebellion event. This conflict lasted over a year, and the British had to send in troops to put down the rebellion. What the ruling elite learned changed the course of American history, but it also changed the direction of the world and its unfolding history forever.

Being outnumbered, the ruling elite came to recognize that, to prevent this sort of incident from happening again, they had to redefine and change the social structure of society. They had to divide the masses so that the majority would align with them without being at the same status level. They had in common with the majority of European immigrants like them because they had the same skin complexion.

Even though we know there is no such thing as "white people," and "pink" would have been more accurate to describe their actual complexion, the term "white" was their choice for more deviant reasons. And the majority of the common people "drank the Kool-Aid." The word "white" carried the definitive connotation of pure, innocent, clean, and stainless. That is precisely what they wanted to imply to the people as a sell, as an appeal to enroll others in their dastardly scheme vastly. "Whiteness" as a classification for people was born out of fear. This is why, even to this day, the promotion of "whiteness" is engulfed in fear, ignorance, and subsequent violence.

Our effort in this book is to make it plain and clear that there is a cost to human life in living a life not based on or grounded in the truth. There comes a time when a person will pay anything they have in their possession to

The Healing of the African American Soul

restore their health. For many, this sense of urgency comes too late, at least in their minds, to reverse the course.

We are at a point in our healing crisis that we must decide, we as descendants of the enslaved Africans and the so-called "white" people, as well as the world community at large, whether we truly want to stop the bleeding of what is in our best social interest and our human concerns for each other; or do we decide to allow narrow self-interest and selfish greed to cause us to bleed ourselves, our healthy social and mutual interest to death.

We are at a time like no other time in human history, and the truth is clear for those who want to or are willing to see it. There is no religion, no elite class, no special people, or any other kind of created entity that has a monopoly on truth. It is in the open and available for all to claim as our G-d given rightful possession and ownership. What is truth?

It is the nature we are constructed on; we live in truth when we are in harmony with nature. Living in truth means we are sincere, living without pretense. This is the case because words spoken in truth carry a higher frequency, elevating our spiritual being and natural humanness. As a true human being, the only way I can have the best life for myself is to establish the best and most excellent life for all other human beings.

"If you light a lamp to show the path for someone else, it will also brighten your own path."
Buddhist Proverb

The Healing of the African American Soul
Belief

2016, Collin Kaepernick took a knee, because of his own belief.
He knew his people were overdue for an abundance of relief.
Relief from the tyranny of those who took an oath to protect and to serve,
But instead, they got unjust treatment that no human being would deserve.
2020, police officer Derek Chauvin also took a knee because of his belief.
For what he had in his mind, he too, desperately wanted relief.
He wanted relief from the perceived threat to his white identity.
So, on the neck of George Floyd, he took a knee for what seemed to be eternity.
For a full 8 minutes and 46 seconds he used his license to kill,
While the world watched, as 8 minutes and 46 seconds of time stood still.
2020, a large crowd of people peacefully gathered at the capital for belief.
They came from around this great land to share the demand that the descendants of slaves get relief.
Cognitive dissonance would no longer allow them to sit quiet and idly by.
Seeing fellow human beings consistently, intently, without mercy, unnecessarily die.
Slain at the hands of a system that is duty bound to protect and to serve.
Instead, they received cruelty, injustice and treatment that they did not deserve.

The Healing of the African American Soul

They were met by an overwhelming force, equipped in riot gear.
They were gassed, arrested and thrown in jail so the president could make it real clear.
To show the perceived threat to prevailing white privilege could not take place now and here, He tried to reassure the fox news viewer they certainly had nothing to fear.
January 6, 2021, another capital crowd gathered largely because of belief.
They too sought relief, from what they had been told and exuding from the tongue of a thief.
It was not the theft of an election that would have them so much aggrieved.
As it was the theft of their identity of white privilege that they had been conditioned to perceive.
They were told by the president and his mighty men that everything is on the line,
And you have a right to fight and to force them to make wrong, right this time.
Let's have trial by combat, and then let's kick ass and take names,
The potent emotion in the obvious lie, sent the passion of the crowd into flames.
They were sent to the capital with nothing "peaceful" in mind,
but no overwhelming police force in riot gear this time.
With obvious help from way up high the people's house was attacked and overrun.
They were intent and determined to have the representative elections of the year 2020, undone.
These people were motivated by their belief!
They bought the lie, that the other guy was the thief!

The Healing of the African American Soul

Why, Biden and Harris were in the camp of their enemy!
Warnock and Ossoff, oh, no! That just cannot be!
These would-be patriots were played by a professional con!
Anything that came out of his mouth they would take it and run!
Trump knew how to speak to what deep down in the heart these people believed!
Even thou he and his mighty band knew from the beginning that these folks were deceived!
To be partners in the slave maker's willful scheme!
With the lure of achieving the American dream!
Even thou, in reality they were not far removed!
From the people they had been conditioned to vehemently disapprove!
These people have been fed and branded with the big lie!
The pink skin, they were tricked to call white was staged to give them a social get by!
At the price of their true humanity, they went right along!
Siding with the liars, while in their hearts they knew it was dead wrong!
To receive benefits, not based on the merit of anything they had done!
Confronting this reality is just mentally no fun!
These people were called deplorables since they were no more than pawns in the master's game! They were duped and grouped into claiming "white" as their name!
They brought the monstrous, destructive white lie, that so-called white skin is enough in this world to get by!

The Healing of the African American Soul

But now that this lie has run its course!
The truth is marching, building and gaining in force!
America, the time for you is now at hand!
The Creator of justice is in full command!
America, on the side of truth you must take your stand!
Choose wrong and you too, will be buried in the sand!
Wali Sabir *1/25/2021*

Real Relief

Belief is a part of the natural design.
Belief is a tool to grow and mature the human mind.
Belief when consistent with The Creator's plan,
Evolves the true human to an up-right stand.
But human perfection can't exist with choice!
So, it's with free will that human creation is given a voice!
Belief as a tool can be used to advance and grow human civilization!
Or it can be used to bring about unthinkable chaos and inhuman devastation!
Belief in the possession of a mature mind can bring relief!
Belief in the possession of an immature mind, is no more than a thief!
The Creator created everything in truth! And in the assertions of the thief, natures provide no proof!
Relief cannot be, just based on how you feel, When what you feel is actually not real.
Not real in context with the reality.
Reality being what the Creator intended life to be.
"Be" is from the verb "to be" that is a command,
lief or spelled leaf, is in essence "life."

The Healing of the African American Soul

This is seen in the story of Adam and his wife.
To be fruitful, abundant and multiply By
Submitting to truth and not buying the lie.
The thief, that gave the world the biggest lie ever told!
The deadly lie that has corrupted men and women at the foundation of their heart and soul.
Men and women that see themselves as decent and upstanding human beings!
But they bought the lie to objectify, making the human beings no more than things!
Belief in the superiority of whiteness is beyond just a lie,
It is a false social construct, crafted to deceive, designed to defy.
Defy the law of how creation is to ebb and to flow.
It brings about an environment where men refuse to know and to grow.
Blinded by their intent and material greed,
Lies are what they manufacture and on that, they feed.
They propagate lies and sow deceit,
It is truth that they are determined to bury and defeat.
Just think about how, in what court can you defend!
A system that is set up to run on something as shallow as skin.
Where Character determined solely, by the flesh you are in!
Now the only way you can get the people to buy this lie,
Their sense of self you must redefine and objectify.
The material is said to be no more than 2% of who we are.
So, staking one's identity on that, is going way, way too far.
The world is upside down and turning on this big lie.

The Healing of the African American Soul
And on this false premise men, women and children, too frequently die.
Die because of false belief!
Die because they are blind to relief!
Relief that is in the Creator's natural plan, to grow and evolve into the true hu-man.

Wali Sabir
1/25/2021
Elevate Your Expectation

When you are consumed with yesterday
Your present never comes your way.
When the lower brain is where you stay
To your future you have no say
Without a plan, what come what may.
Human potential goes astray.
But in your hand is your own clay
To mold and fashion your best day
Come alive in your higher mind.
Don't let the pass keep you behind.
Become grounded in your reality.
Let your true presence set you free.
We are born with what we need.
To nurture and to grow our seed.
With well-made plans for tomorrow Let your work today be without sorrow.
We don't come a running before crawling.
Success will come after some falling.
So, get up, stand up and stay in the race.
Let your aims and goal determine your pace.
Elevate your own expectation.
Fueled by healthy imagination.

The Healing of the African American Soul
You are not born in a nature of sin.
You are born in excellence, in order to win!

Wali Sabir

Chapter 2: Our Soul in Crisis

"Nothing can dim the light which shines from within."
Maya Angelou

We come into this world with no "say so" regarding our ethnicity, our height, the hue of our skin, the color of our eyes, or many other biological traits. There is nothing specific about our basic biology that would make one person better or worse than another person. Proof of this is that some people would say from a surface view that they have a physical handicap. Still, upon a closer look, you will find that the so-called handicap is actually a blessing that has been leveraged into awakenings and outstanding achievements for that persons being.

The point is, the material world is inanimate, without a soul, and cannot be blamed for the atrocities perpetrated in its name. One would be hard-pressed to find one individual that has not been impacted by the misappropriation of skin tone as a value to rate and equate human beings. When this is done, the result is that the soul of the human being is wounded, demoralized, and traumatized. Some seem to be less affected than others by this grave injury; however, in many respects, because of their insensitivities, they are actually the worse off. In this book, it is our primary goal to look at the wounding and the healing of the soul of American descendants of the formerly enslaved people.

I believe, though, that a careful inspection of <u>the sojourning process</u> that has injured the soul of the enduring, formerly enslaved African people <u>epitomizes</u>,

The Healing of the African American Soul

and is in fact, the essential and true unfoldment at the heart of the true American story; as opposed to the unfair, discriminating rationalization of "his-story." In the past, "his-story" (as opposed to the actual story) monopolized the airwaves, pressurizing the environment, and the prevailing powerbrokers effectively controlled how their message was crafted and delivered to the unsuspecting public. As the story goes, the lion will always be the victor until the prey becomes the story's narrator.

I am of the formerly enslaved Americans, and the ink that flows in these pages is wreaked from the social blood of my injured soul. America is truly the greatest country on earth today, while at the same time, the sickest country on earth today. America is great because she incorporated the greatness of The Creator in the language of her founding. Also, those incorporated words relating to principles of excellence applied to the sacredness of the human being have protected, preserved, and perpetuated profound ideals, at least conceptually; and those ideals still advance hope and the foundational potential driving the aspiration of pursuing human excellence. While at the same time, the prominent evil of greed and dominance is co-existing and has been ruling the day.

Enslavement and its aftermath ensued, and hundreds of years of free slave labor indeed ushered in American materialistic greatness. And American Hisstory, as it continuously unfolds, has been giving herself over to the support of some preponderant subhuman drives and consequential influences. And the only way America can be whole is to face the undeniable reality of the true American story.

The true American story began with social objectification of the original human being through the ill-

The Healing of the African American Soul

treatment and classification of skin color, skin tone, and skin complexion.

Human skin is the outer covering of the body and is the largest organ of the integumentary system. Because it interfaces with the environment, skin plays an important immunity role in protecting the body against pathogens and excessive water loss. Its other functions are insulation, temperature regulation, sensation, synthesis of vitamin D, and protection of vitamin B folates.

While the skin plays such a vital role in our physical well-being, its role in our social and emotional well-being runs significantly below the conscious radar. More than any other human organ, skin has a profound and far-reaching impact on the socio-economic climate in the world today. The objectification of skin as a label for human identity has been weaponized. Skin color has become an instrument of mass destruction, scattering the environment with multitudes of injured souls.

Our natural creation is truly marvelous in every respect. For instance, nature has a built-in process that kicks in right away to deal with any injury when a wounding occurs. In case of a wound to the skin, an overlapping four-stage process called the **cascade of healing** goes to work at once. This is nature's attempt to restore normal structure and function to remediate the wound.

Wound healing involves two distinct functions, regeneration and repair. Some wounds where regeneration is required and some where repair is needed, depending on the wound's type and severity. The body is impressive in its innate intelligence in the discernment of which principle to apply. Which function would *you* think is more applicable to affect healing for our wounded and traumatized souls?

The Healing of the African American Soul

There is a saying that "success leaves clues." Our biological makeup and function prove to be very successful how The Creator Has designed it. Therefore, the principles in wound healing on the natural biological level can be very instructive on the psychological and social levels.

As ex-slaves, if there ***was*** one word, the one word that can indeed sum up our total experience in America is "Wounded." The evidence of our wounds can be seen in every withering aspect of our lives. And to this day, there has been no honest, meaningful, conscious attempt specifically designed to holistically regenerate or repair our wounds.

So, as a direct consequence, there are no people on the face of this earth that is more unestablished than the African descendants of slaves. African Americans are some of the most outstanding Americans and human beings who have ever lived but have no collective social establishment as a people. To address our wound healing or the lack thereof, we must shift our paradigm of thought. In scripture, Prophet Solomon is advised to take a hint from the ants. It would be wise of us to take a fresh look at the patterns that The Creator Established in creation as proven models for guidance on dealing with our social and emotional wounds.

We, the descendants of the formerly enslaved, are the products of a 400-year journey, moving through this North American experiment, being subjected to one walloping wound right after another, in the wake of one of the greatest crimes in history. We have been on this path through chattel slavery, Jim Crow, oppression, repression, aggression, segregation, and inner-self subjugation, as the

The Healing of the African American Soul

selected channels fostering the subject's objectives: to objectify people.

The theme in this dreadful drama has been to reduce human beings to mere soulless objects. The direct impact for us as ex-slaves is that we, although distinct individuals, make up a collective soul experience. That is, after 400 years of being in the greatest country on earth, we as a people have not justifiably improved our lot. They ask, why do we have the highest rates of morbidity, dysfunctionality, and mortality? Why do we make up almost 40% of the prison population while we are only 13% of the total U.S. population? Further, they ask, why after 400 years, in the biggest economy in the world, do we own no more than 2% of the country's wealth?

Each one of these social indicators suggests that, indeed, we are a people in a severe crisis. A crisis is described as a time of intense difficulty or trouble. A crisis could also suggest that a significant injury has happened. In our particular case, we have been wounded and traumatized by the worst form of slavery and complete degradation in human history. We were damaged physically, yes, but that is not the worst injury perpetrated upon us.

The physical wounds pale in comparison to our psychological wounds. As slaves, we were taken out of our natural environment and robbed of our normal and natural support systems for our physical, emotional, and spiritual well-being. We were captives in an environment that made us the legal animalistic property of another man. To add misery and suffering to inflicted pain, an environment was created to systematically support every negative attribution

The Healing of the African American Soul

derogated and assigned to the enslaved people by the oppressors.

This book wants to look at slavery from a supernumerary perspective as a systematic process to inflict deep, long-lasting psychological wounds. Slavery was terrorism and subhuman cruelty in the worst sort of way that drew a lot of physical blood. We are still bleeding physically from the effects of slavery. The blood we draw from each other is from police killings of unarmed "black" men. The blood of Eugenics, in the name of population control. The blood from sickness and death through water contamination, healthy food and nutrition deprivation, medical apartheid and experiments, social, environmental injustices perpetrated in our targeted community, and so on. But more important than the imposition of all of that, slavery pierced our minds and spilled our inner psychological blood.

The blood of our emotional and social intelligence is hemorrhaging at life-threatening rates. This blood loss shows up in our misguided social interaction with ourselves and our natural environment. We have lost the connection with our environment to the point that we do not adequately sustain ourselves from it. Is this "state of being" resultant from and related to our inability to trust our social environment in America fully? In 400 years, we have not established a level of collective social intelligence organized so that we have been able to stop the mass bleeding. There is mainly something keeping us in this perpetual healing crisis.

Our physical injuries naturally set into motion this automatic series of events often referred to biologically as the **"cascade of healing,"** to repair or regenerate the injured tissues. The cascade of **healing** is divided into

The Healing of the African American Soul

these four (4) overlapping **phases**: Hemostasis, Inflammatory, Proliferative, and Maturation.

In the first phase of hemostasis, the number one priority is to stop the bleeding. In the second phase, the task is cleaning the wound and killing the bacteria. The third phase is focused on replenishing and covering the wound. During the Maturation, the fourth phase, the new tissue slowly gains strength and flexibility. Here, in the maturation phase, collagen fibers reorganize, the tissue remodels, gets sturdier, and matures, and there is an overall increase in tensile strength.

The physical side of our wounds has healed through these natural processes, but there is a spiritual, logical sentiment side to these wounds. Here, I refer to these wounds as social wounds or psychological wounds. These wounds run very deep, and they manifest in all manners of dysfunctions reflected in the indicators mentioned above. These wounds and their underlying causes have never been addressed and redressed with the seriousness they truly warrant and deserve.

During the American Reconstruction Period, one of the first attempts at bending the arch of justice to the formerly enslaved. This effort was overshadowed and dwarfed by an evil black code, Jim Crow social era that even eclipsed physical bondage and made the cruelty of slavery look like child's play. We are still experiencing the remnants of that social era in the 21st Century.

In the book "The Color of Money," Mehrsa Baradaran substantiates the story of President Lyndon B. Johnson, being the closest U.S. president ever, coming to reckon with the history of racial injustice. Johnson expressively said to an African American audience at Howard University that "America had failed the Negro and

The Healing of the African American Soul

that freedom was not enough." "You do not take a person who, for years, has been hobbled by chains and then liberate him, bring him up to the starting line of a race and then say, you are free to compete (equally) with all the others, and still justly believe (in your mind) that you have been completely fair."

President Johnson is noted for the articulated efforts of his administration's War on Poverty. But, like the attempts to right wrongs during the reconstruction era, Johnson's War on Poverty was eclipsed, overshadowed, and occulted by the War on Crime. The War on Crime was a label put on an upgraded strategy for Jim Crow, called the Southern Strategy. This strategy, in a nutshell, blamed the victim for being the victim, and the result was mass incarceration and an uptick in the total disenfranchisement of the formerly enslaved community. So, we are still bleeding from these wounds, such erratic, unreliable, unsustained programs that we can readily identify as our social healing crisis, or the lack thereof.

I believe, just as there is a cascade of healing for our material self, that same pattern is true for our nonmaterial self. These principles, if applied correctly, can be the key to the healing of our injured soul. Slavery, as stated above, drew a lot of physical blood. Blood being a life force, the slave owners did not want to draw too much blood to render their property useless. They only wanted to draw enough physical blood to produce, initiate and cause the perpetuation of the psychological or social bleeding.

They had to reverse the natural process in the cascade of healing to draw the psychological or social blood. As stated, the first phase in the cascade of healing is Hemostasis. This phase begins at the onset of injury, and the objective is to stop the bleeding. Here the body activates its emergency repair system, the blood clotting system, and

The Healing of the African American Soul

forms a dam to block the drainage. During this healing process, platelets come into contact with collagen, and it initiates the formation of a fibrin mesh, strengthening the platelet clumps into a stable clot.

To understand how they reverse the process, we must first understand the psychological or social blood. Let us revisit the concept or legend of definition. I refer to this blood as our **common sense**. Common is described as a shared practice, civil behavior, or accepted social concerns based on respect for natural, innate, or born intelligence.

Common sense, in this context, is not something that you have to go to school to get. Sense is described as the faculty by which the body perceives an external stimulus. In other words, through the window of our five senses, sight, hearing, smell, taste, and touch, we bring in external information to relate to and adjust the internal reality with the external reality. When this adjustment is based on accurate sense perception, sound judgment can be achieved.

Sound judgment is dynamically influenced, keeping us present in the here and now while allowing us to benefit from the past, but with greater interest looking to the resulting future. By resulting future, we mean a better future because we make better choices in the present. To make a useful slave, the system of slavery had to focus on dulling the senses of the enslaved people. Systematic conditioning on the conscious and subconscious levels. For the slave, sound judgment had to be only a matter of an objective for survival and not one for consideration for the natural aspiration of human dignity.

As a life force, the blood brings in nutrients and removes contaminants from the body. Inside the social blood, our common sense is our natural inclination to be

The Healing of the African American Soul

upright, that is, to do the right thing, as we perceive it. When our thinking and actions are based on pure and honorable intentions, our common sense is equipped with the principles and values that allow us to better discern between right and wrong.

The key to our common sense's health is not in the rightness or wrongness of our choice at the moment because, as perfect humans, we will not always make the best choices. Naturally, humans grow, mature, and learn from their mistakes. The most important thing is our intentions; our intentions are our natural capacity for perfection as ascending human beings. Through the proper functioning of our five senses, our pure intentions bring in the good nutrients and remove the contaminants from our social life.

Under the scheme of the social manipulators, the social blood was set up to work with a fractured sense body. Instead of five senses, the enslaved people were trained and conditioned to use only three of the five senses. The motor senses of sight and hearing were factored out. This pattern can also be seen in another example, in what was constructed as the slave diet.

A balanced diet consists of five things, minerals, vitamins, proteins, carbohydrates, and fats. The slave diet mainly consisted of the latter three, proteins, carbohydrates, and fats. The slave diet was not constructed based on what is wholesome and nutritionally beneficial. The only consideration was for providing enough energy for the enslaved to do the work. Likewise, in the "slave food" diet, a great deal of the vitamins and minerals were factored out. This is consistent with the true meaning of the 3/5 person.

The Healing of the African American Soul

It is impossible to have accurate sense perception if you only work with three of your five senses. When the higher motor senses are removed, what is left is a creature of feeling, thus, the defined term, "spook." Emotions, when they are not connected to spiritual insight that grounds us in our own reality, it leaves us with a base focused on the physical.

Therefore, our social blood of common sense is contaminated, mixing falsehood with truth. Thus, the good nutrients, like honesty, humility, sincerity, and constancy, become so watered down that lies, superstition, weak ideas, and wrong thinking take up space in our mind. The result is that we become consumed with physical, biological, materialistic-centered living, vibrating by design, in the lower regions of the mind.

We now know, based on science, that words are compelling. The words we speak and the words expressed in our environment can shape and fashion our decisions and our DNA. It has been scientifically revealed that the intent behind them most impacts the frequency of words. And the context and method by which the message in the words is delivered are also of great significance. This explains how we can be a spiritually based people on the one hand and be conditioned to be materially focused on the other. People can know that there is more to life than what they can smell, feel and touch, the 3/5's person, but the words they hear that programs their life distort the reality of what they actually see.

Masaru Emoto (1943 – 2014) was a Japanese researcher who had dedicated his life to the "language" of the water. What he discovered is something significant: water has a memory and can **store information.** You can take two glasses of water, speak words of peace and love to one and speak words of hate and madness to the other and

The Healing of the African American Soul

freeze them both; the crystals that form in each of them are according to what you speak, manifested into visible reality. The crystals formed in words of peace and love are organized in beauty, order, and harmony. The crystals formed in words of hate and madness are disorganized, chaotic, and very unattractive.

The human being is composed of approximately 76.2 % water. Think about it. We, the formerly enslaved people, have been in a hostile Word environment for over 400 years. Words of hate and ill will that are spoken to and against us by people, with the social power and the legal authority to act on them, have been and still are, to a great extent, a part of our total reality. I believe it is only our natural, spiritual-based inclination that has saved us from total self-destruction.

However, as creatures of feeling, we need "things" to feel good, but that feel-good feeling is short-lived because you can never have enough "things" to feel good permanently. The social manipulators had to materialize the public to make their scheme work. They materialize the European people as white, but that was not their most deviant magic trick. They also purported god as white; when I was growing up, I thought he was white. Everything with power in the society was white, and they showed me a picture of a white man and said he was god, and I was convinced and believed them.

In actuality, the language of "whiteness" is a big lie that is borne out of fear. A lie by its nature means to deny the truth, which is the same as to deny reality. So, despite our best effort to be correct and do the right thing, we have been climbing a ladder to discover that ladder is leaning against the wrong wall. This is a concocted wall built on a foundation of lies. We were climbing a material wall, reaching for a material white god on the top of that wall.

The Healing of the African American Soul

The white man on top of that wall spoke words that created an environment of tyranny and vile subhuman behavior. Words that spoke into being violent lynching's, murder, burning alive, castrations, cross burnings, home bombings, church bombings, town burnings, drawing red lines around our communities, casting a web of poverty all over America wherever we live, voting in laws that disenfranchise us, oppressive profiling, convict leasing, police killings, human astigmatism and so on and so forth. African American suffrage became the law of the land in America.

We, the ex-enslaved people, are severely wounded. Our social and emotional blood is running like flowing water. We are grateful, a very spiritual people, and our sincere love for The Creator is what has preserved us under the most trying and dehumanizing conditions. But we are also checked and held back from authentic establishment and liberation because of our attachment to the roots of contrived, artificial whiteness.

Whiteness is a "spell," and the world has been put under "the spell of whiteness." But no one is more impacted by it than we, the American descendants of the formerly enslaved people. No, we do not call ourselves "white," but we do call ourselves "black." Black and white are opposites. The problem with calling ourselves black is that black as a label for social identity is a reaction to the "lie" of whiteness. This means we are giving whiteness control over who we say we are. That is, per se, the very objective of social whiteness, which is, in fact, to be in control.

Every measure of our success that can be pointed to is a fractured success. Regardless of the amount of money or the recognizable fame, we have not produced any actual achievements. True success cannot be achieved on an individual basis. We are social beings, and that means we

The Healing of the African American Soul

must be established socially for success. Would that not be just? Who is it, in human form, that would fear injustice? Our Social establishment means we must establish productive, progressive, structured, and balanced community life. Does the oppressor really see the oppressed as self-subsistent while he, himself, is subsistent upon us? Ever since slavery, most of our collective action has been on what oppression we are against. We are against the lynching, we are against discrimination, we stand against all injustice to all, but true establishment is not built on what you are against; it is built on what you are standing up for.

Slave language, as manifested through slave culture, has reduced the worldview to a physical visual of black and white. It is a world of extremes, good-bad, love-hate, have-have nots, upper-lower, and of course, everything positive is defined as "white." Whiteness is the elephant in the room because it is all-consuming, but no one notices it, it seems. Why do people, by and large, fear even openly discuss it? It is established as the yardstick by which everything is measured. Therefore, when you do not measure up to the rule of whiteness in the slave culture, one must work inwardly against it; at least, you have to be kinetically reactionary.

To establish productive community life, we must have some idea of how that would look. Productive is from the verb produce, which is described as "to make or manufacture from components or raw material." In other words, we must be engaged with our natural environment. This is necessary to bring out of it that which is helpful for our maintenance and progressive development in the establishment of model community life.

We are created and made from the earth, so going into the earth is like going into ourselves. It is reported that the

The Healing of the African American Soul

last Prophet, upon him be peace, said: "He who has known himself has known his Creator." It stands to reason that to know self, one must understand what they are made of. The unnatural "word environment" of slave culture caused us to have an unnatural relationship with our earth (ourselves). Therefore, we could not come to know ourselves nor our Creator.

It has been stated that the relationship that one has with ones' Creator is the relationship upon which all other relationships are based. Suppose the frequency of the words used that form this most crucial relationship is from our natural environment. In that case, it can only reflect the love and caring that the Creator Establishes for His entire creation. The Creator never created a thing without that thing having everything it requires and needs to sustain itself.

We see that minerals in the creation came before plants, plants came before animals, and all of these came before the human being. As managers or custodians of the creation, the human being must know the creation and his role as a manager in the creation. To establish productive community life, as custodians, they must know their relationship with every part of the creation and how to maintain the balance between one thing and another.

In reality, our present life is reflective and looks just like the pictures we have in our minds. So, if we don't like what we see of ourselves, we have to change the definitive words that shape the pictures we have in our own minds. Changing our "word diet" is what will help stop the social bleeding. The language we need to accomplish this must be morally and principle-based and a language of repetition and high frequency. It shall not be the language that puts us under the spell of whiteness, a language of low frequency.

The Healing of the African American Soul

While we all have our unique individual purpose, we also have a collective purpose, as well. We have a shared goal in our soul of establishing model human community life. Community is "coming into unity." Coming into unity is a picture that reflects a group of people who command at least all their five senses. Such common command allows us to be grounded based on our own reality. Being grounded in our own reality is a mandated social necessity for us and is not the reaction to the existence of "whiteness."

Pursuing the bestowed excellence of our human nature is the only way we can be present in our own reality, and the only way we can be self-reliant is to be present and in the reality of the moment. To create such a reality for ourselves, for the ex-enslaved people, we must apply the principles established in the cascade of healing as a guideline to heal our injured soul.

First, we will look at the social blood, using the clues in the biological blood to give us insight into its significance in the life and well-being of the body as a whole. As pointed out scientifically, the blood is made of four components, *plasma, red blood cells, white blood cells, and platelets*. These four distinctions parallel multiple sets of four in our psychological or social construction. The first set of fours that we will consider are *material, emotional, intellectual, and spiritual*.

In scripture, it is stated that "the first will be last and last, will be first." In the case of this set of four, it is the spiritual or spirit that is last. So, conversely, in the context of this reality, it is to be first. The spirit manifests through the material, then expresses itself with emotion, and grows in intelligence to be a complete spiritual human being. We also see this through the evolution of our thought process, from the lower *reptilian brain to the limbic brain, to the*

The Healing of the African American Soul

neocortex or higher brain. The fourth and highest development is that of the *pineal organ.*

It is the first organ to form and from which all other organ develops in the amazing fetus. The pineal organ is also said to be the focus in the study of our spiritual development. However, just like our spiritual life has been materialized, the pineal organ is materialized through calcification. The extent to which this calcification impacts our spiritual development is not known, but we know it does not help the development.

We are bleeding social blood because our common sense has been materialized. Think about it! For over 400 years, we have been consuming a word diet that says The Creator is white. Like in a good movie, they build the set to make it look natural, the actors are dressed up, and they all know their lines. The stage is set. Everyone in the movie is in character; even ex-slaves are in character because our roles are spontaneously performed. Our part is a reaction to a well-rehearsed and calculated plan of the conspiring, image-building slave makers.

Our existence in this staged drama is an artificial materialized reality, using a grafted mentality, void of the responsibility to establish and maintain a productive community life for ourselves. And it plays out to the letter. As our blood circulates through our body and delivers essential substances like oxygen and nutrients to its cells, it transports metabolic waste products from those living cells. Like the blood that circulates through our biology, a life force circulates through our psychology.

I relate this life force to **social intelligence**. The thing that best describes social intelligence is our **common sense**. When our common sense functions correctly, it circulates through our community life, both the individual

The Healing of the African American Soul

community of inner self and the collective community of outer selves, our human society. Common sense delivers values and principles like honesty, humility, and sincerity to our community life in its correct form. It is also common sense that identifies waste and other harmful materials and helps us dispose of them.

The social manipulators set up a structure to emphasize material-centered thinking than mental and spiritual balance. Because everything in creation operates on a prescribed frequency and vibration, material matter operates at a lower frequency than spiritual phenomena in higher forms. According to their design, the social manipulators created a supportive language environment based on low vibrations to materialize the human being.

The domain of the reptilian brain, where the focus is on survival concerns, is targeted. At this level of functionality, the creature is said to be cold-blooded and lacking in the warmth of social intercourse and sensitivities. Their objective was to materialize the human being by making the natural unnatural; they said man was born "in sin" because the natural act of marital relations (sexual intercourse) is defined in their language design as sinful. They made the Creator a man and put him in white skin. These are the concepts and ideas in the foundation of the social structure on which the cultural walls have been built in a design to objectify humanity.

Like blood circulates in our body, our social blood or common sense must have four vital social institutions that allow the human community to survive and thrive. Through these social institutions, specialized organs are established to address the needs of the individual, the family, and the community.

The Healing of the African American Soul

They collectively must be structured in ways that maintain the balance in the best interest of all. They are namely: education, economics, governance, and culture, which are another set of the four parallels in the social blood. Through these social institutions, the individual's life, the family, and the community are addressed and regulated. All the things required in human life that involve the interaction and inter-relationships of one human being with another are supported. Like our body organs, these institutions should function to circulate the social intelligence of common sense, promoting the balance necessary for sustainable natural human community life.

The object of slavery was to make life unnatural under the false pretense of being natural and moral in its structured makeup. Therefore, there had to be a philosophical justification in the social framework for instituting slavery. To justify slavery, the enslaved people had to be redefined and made non-human. To make the enslaved people non-human, the slave makers themselves had to become sub-human.

Again, words make people. The slave culture created a word environment that simultaneously spills the blood of social intelligence of both the victim and the victimizer. The language of slave culture continuously deepens the wounds and prevents the natural process of social hemostasis from working for us and actually from ever taking place. Our social wounds are very much a part of our personal and social reality, and we are still profusely bleeding.

Had we been in a natural environment, the first step would have been to stop the social bleeding. But slave culture is un-natural; we must understand that slavery was an environment where we had to deny our common sense. To survive, we had to take on a false common sense, deny our humanity, and function like a domesticated animal to

The Healing of the African American Soul

merely survive. Our common, natural interest as a people was always secondary and subordinate to the slave master's material interest.

An excellent example of this during the enslavement period of Africans in America is outlined in the "Meritorious Manumission Act" of 1710. This **legalized governmental** act was enacted in Virginia. It was the legal act of freeing a slave for so-called "good deeds," as the national public policy defined it, and could be granted to a slave, thusly: who saved the life of a White master or his property, who invented something from which a slave master could make a profit, or who "snitched" on a fellow slave who was planning a slave rebellion or to run away. Every effort was made to ensure that the four institutions of social blood were used against us, to keep us unestablished, keeping our social blood spilling on the streets in our healing crisis.

Education as a natural social phenomenon is designed to bring out the unique gifts that are encoded in human intelligence, waiting to be brought out through proper cultivation. Every human being comes into life with **DNA, Divine-Natural-Ability**. Slavery created a system where we were under Constance attack to deny our DNA. There is no better example than this: John Henry Berry, in the Virginia House, said, *"Sir, we have, as far as possible closed every avenue by which light might enter their mind; we have only to go one step further—to extinguish the capacity (for them) to see the light, and our work would be completed; they would then be reduced to the level of the beasts of the field, and we should be safe; and I am not certain that we would not do it if we could find out the necessary process — and that under the plea of necessity."*

The Healing of the African American Soul

The slave makers used their institutions to brand in through education and indoctrination, the non-human status of the enslaved people. While at the same time elevating this newly created identity of "white" to *superhuman* and even believing they are a superior race and "god-like." For indeed, they claim the power of life and death over the enslaved people. The extreme measures they took to produce a language environment to reflect this fabricated doctrine were all-consuming. Education, or better yet, miss-education was used to deepen the wound further. So, phases two, three, and four of the social healing never had a chance to play their role. We are still bleeding.

I want to applaud the work of Brian Stevenson at this time and express my gratitude to him for his work in the area of equal justice. His work is truly groundbreaking in addressing the rigged system of social injustice.

Another person I want to point to is Shawn Rochester and his book "Black tax." I will address more about him later.

Also, Mehrsa Baradaran and her outstanding work in her book "The Color of Money." Their impeccable research and scholarship are a game-changer in understanding the root cause and perpetuation of the wealth gap between the formerly enslaved people and the so-called white people. Their works document the manifestation of Henry Berry's words, mentioned above, in the Virginia House in 1832. These are some of the contributions to inform the public in ways to check the social bleeding.

Economics, as a component of our social intelligence, requires keen insight between wants and needs. We *want* food, clothing, and shelter; we also *need* food, clothing, and shelter. We want safety, security, and

The Healing of the African American Soul

peace of mind. We also need protection, security, and peace of mind. The original meaning of economics is the management of the household. How we meet our needs in balance with our wants is the key to good management. Slave culture and the established norms were nonsupportive of the formerly enslaved people's effort to do for themselves. We can point to example after example where we were making positive strives toward self-reliance, just to have those efforts come under attack, destroyed, and rendered dead.

This system has always promoted that the formerly enslaved be in a state of wishing and wanting. As a social creature, we naturally wish for and want to be accepted and integrated into society like everyone else. Dr. King's idea of civil rights was not the idea of integration that was broadly promoted. The idea of integration that is mainly promoted is one that I call intersubjugation. He did not just want a seat at the lunch counter; he wanted a seat in the board room where decisions are made.

He wanted an integration more like what was proposed by Andrew Brimmer. Andrew Brimmer, as Mehrsa Baradaran points out in her book, "was born to a family of sharecroppers in Louisiana, received his Ph.D. in economics from Harvard, and was appointed by President Johnson as the first black governor of the Federal Reserve in 1966." He stated, "The only promising path to equal opportunity for Negroes in business as in other aspects of economic activity, lies in full participation in an intergraded, national economy."

Instead of inclusion, we were duped into reacting to exclusion, like in the practice of consuming those glittering things that would make us feel that we were more socially acceptable. Those things that we think will elevate our status or the things that will bring us closer to whiteness.

The Healing of the African American Soul

We want our hair to be like white hair; we rate our sense of beauty on what is more Euro-centric. Our economy is geared around wishing and wanting to be more like white. Here again, whiteness is the elephant in the room. This is what we mean when we say that we are not grounded in our own reality. We, the ex-slave people, bleed profusely in this domain as it relates to our social intelligence.

Our wants are nowhere close to being in balance with our needs. As an example, we have individual intelligence to get many of the things we want as individuals. But what we need also is group intelligence if we're going to be established in the human community. Our economics awareness, as it relates to money, resources, industry, and employment, was always about how we fit into someone else's plan for us.

When it comes to economics, our sense of management is non-sense. Over a trillion dollars pass through our hands every year, and we do not retain 2% of that income. We have the highest unemployment rate with the same human needs and concerns as other people, yet we do not convert our needs and concerns into businesses that meet our needs and provide employment for ourselves. Slavery conditioned us to depend on a slave master for our overall well-being and not trust our own D.N.A., Divine Natural Abilities.

We are conditioned to distrust the most valuable resource we have: our relationships with each other. We have heard it all, "a nigger can't do nothing for me. Don't nigger rig it. I don't do business with black people; they ain't got it together." We are wounded, and to the degree that we do not measure up economically to other businesses, we have lost sight of exactly why that is the case.

The Healing of the African American Soul

We seem not to understand that it is by design, and until we consciously break the cycle, we will always be in this perpetuated state. Just as long as we make our judgments and decisions on the surface of things and not rooted in the ground of our own truthful reality, we will continue to make shallow, superficial, and unsound choices. Wisdom says that sometimes, you have to take a step back to take two steps ahead. This concept can be personified in the metaphysical African Sankofa bird.

Our traumatized soul is in absolute crisis, and our economic behavior is a good indicator to what extent the crisis persists. We must understand that our behavior by design is subject to be reactionary. We are like puppets on a string, being pulled in any direction the puppeteer decides, at his whim. We are programmed to react according to what he has instilled into our synthetically designed makeup. We know that our lack of establishment and social impoverishment is extreme, and the reason we seem to be locked in this state of being is not through happenstance.

The evidence is clear that a big reason for our lack of establishment and the persisting hardships is deliberate and a direct result of layers of government policy. This is not to say we have no culpability in our plight. Although we are not responsible for what is done to us and against us, we are indeed responsible for how we choose to respond to it. That, in fact, is our problem. Our response has not been adequate. A good response is deliberate and carried out with forethought and commitment. We continue to react; a reaction is emotional, impulsive, and void of grounded foresight.

Government represents the political direction, regulation, and control exercised over the actions of the members, officials, citizens or inhabitants of given

The Healing of the African American Soul

communities, societies, and states and management of the resources regarding the affairs of a state, community, etc. - **Government** is necessary to the existence of law and order in a civilized society. The optimal words in this description above of government are direction and control that officials exercised over the actions of the members and the citizens.

This description makes government the most responsible for the plight of the formerly enslaved people of America. As Dr. Jacqueline Battalora points out: "The label "white" reflecting a group of humanity appears nowhere in law until 1681." As we pointed out earlier, white is a reaction created out of fear. But understand, too, that this is a government reaction. The total disenfranchisement of the ex-slaves is a result of direct reactionary policies and laws enacted directly against a targeted population by levels of government.

Also, as we have already stated, Richard Rothstein shows in his book, "The Color of Law," how housing in America was not segregated due to "de facto segregation"; instead, it is a creation of deliberate actions of government. If it *were* a result of a personal choice or an accident, that would be de facto segregation. There is no question that the bottomless pit of poverty and economic isolation in the ghettos of America is a creation of calculated government policies. We pay more for everything, and everything we pay more for is of a lower quality than what the affluent pay less for. We are the most under-served and over-policed people in America; indeed, we are continuously bleeding.

Culture as a social institution reflects the philosophical value systems of a given society as expressed through the arts, cuisine, attire, customs, and other creative manifestations of human intellectual achievement and ascension, regarded in collectivity. People are seen chiefly through their culture. Colonial culture of the early 1600s

The Healing of the African American Soul

was much different than what it gradually morphed into in the 1700s and onward.

As we pointed out earlier, there is growing evidence that the social structure of society was much different, in that everyone was equal under the law, according to their status. All free persons, regardless of their place of origin, had the same legal rights. All persons of indentured status had the same legal rights. Persons of slave status all had the same legal rights. It is a matter of fact that all could earn their way to free status, and slaves were not just the people of African origin. White, as a human label of identity, did not even exist. As we mentioned through this book, whiteness is a creation that reacted out of fear and ignorance. This fear is what has morphed into America's Holocaust against its enslaved Africans and their descendants.

The builders of this new American experiment wanted it to be seen worldwide in the best light. It is evident that there were great thinkers that produced documents like The Declaration of Independence. But they had this problem, and they had this need for cheap labor to take advantage of the vast developing markets of cotton, tobacco, and sugar mainly. These crops required a lot of labor to harvest. As we also pointed out, the masses of ordinary people in the late 1600s were already in unity, protesting against inhuman social conditions. The solution for the elite, who controlled the government, was a strategy to divide and conquer.

The solution of divide and conquer was twofold. First, the elite had to enroll the people that they had the most in common with to be on their side. They accomplished that by creating white as a new false social construct. Secondly, to satisfy the expanding need for a cheap or free labor force, the elite had to dehumanize the people of African origin to

The Healing of the African American Soul

socially justify them being enslaved, abused, and usmyidentifiersThe Healing of the African American Souled for free labor to satisfy their economic demands.

They could not easily reconcile the lofty ideals written in the Constitution like all human beings are created equal with certain inalienable rights, while at the same time executing the cruelty of chattel slavery and the inhuman bondage and treatment that was being inflicted upon the enslaved African people. Therefore, their diabolic criminal scheme against humanity had to be socially justified, so they dressed it up, propped it up, and worked to make it seem that it was the most natural and humane thing to do. Words carry messages that make people, and the influential slave makers understood this well. The biggest trick was played on the European Americans.

They brought the lie of whiteness without being forced, under cover of automatically receiving unearned benefits. The enslaved people were violently forced to exist under the lie of whiteness, while their own humanity had to be repressed to simply survive. A note here, I do not focus on blackness because blackness as a human definition is only a reaction to the false social construct of whiteness. America, as a society, is sick with the disease of whiteness, and the social blood of common sense is flowing unabatedly.

America's Pathology

America's pathology is her historical denial, It's not a new problem, it's been around for a while. For nearly 400 years, your head has been buried in the sand,
Blind to the cruel and inhuman treatment of your fellow man.
America your pathology is your own denial.

The Healing of the African American Soul

Devine justice has you now, on trial.
Yes, you freed me as your chattel slave, But the inhuman condition you preserve, you save.
Even after slavery you had strange fruit hanging from the tree!
While Caucasian men, women and children look on with glee.
America your pathology is your rigid denial.
On Sunday you go to church, you sing, and you smile.
Never reflecting on the backs of the enslaved, you have reached this mile.
America, tell me, how can you stand so aloof?
When it is at your hand the lie became the truth? You weaponized and denigrated human skin, Elevating one, while casting the other in sin.
In fear you gave birth to the classification of white, To scatter the masses in the fear of their own insight.
With the power of law and an artificial social norm, You codified black to be inhuman and a state of deform.
America's pathology is her blatant denial, It's not a new problem, it's been around for a while.
Not one day have you spent on reconciliation and truth, Look at the former enslaved community if you need proof.
We own less than 2% of the nations' wealth,
While we bare more than our share of poverty and poor health.
Our community has no structure to establish and maintain economic enterprise,
So, in crime, many find ways for their skill, intellect and talent to be realized!
America's pathology is her obvious denial, It's not a new problem, it's been around for a while.

The Healing of the African American Soul

As a slave you conditioned me to bow to the awe of your power,
You stacked the deck so my self-initiative would spoil and sour.
You gave favor based on the color of one's skin,
My Blackness was belittled and made an immutable sin.
Yes! America you have been going to church all the while,
And you are still yet, in your pathological denial.
America, tell me, how can you stand so aloof?
Not one day have you stood for reconciliation and truth.
For 250 years you worked me for free,
You took two of my senses and left me with three.
Three fifths of a human being is the brand you put on me.
How then, can you expect me to be whole and be free?
You gave new meaning to what it is to be a pimp,
You broke my leg and complained because I limp.
You made being black the number one crime,
You locked me up for long periods of time.
Working me all day, in each and every way,
Proclaiming to the world, "Niggers ain't got nothing to say."
"Look at how they treat each other,
Brother killing his own brother."
"They won't even support their own kind,
The only thing they share is a bottle of wine."
"They spend more money than many free nations,
Just look at their community, can't you see the devastation?"
"They close down their own businesses, just to sit beside me,
Now tell me how foolish you think niggers can be?"
America's pathology is her evident denial,

The Healing of the African American Soul

It's not a new problem, it's been around for a while.
America are you missing the scheme and the plot.
In the pathology of the ill found wealth that you got.
You cheated, you lied, you murdered, and you stole,
For silver and dollars your humanity was sold.
To live with yourself, you made everything black a natural sin,
The only way you could justify mentally, your evil scheme to win.
America's pathology is her perpetual denial, It's not a new problem, it's been around for a while.
You used your power and influence to redefine the word black,
And none of your social institutions could materially hold back.
They were instructed to treat niggers like a beast, by your will,
And if they don't submit, you are ordered to kill.
America's pathology is her disingenuous denial, It's not a new problem, it's been around for a while.
Now divine justice has you socially and globally on trial.

America, tell me, how can you stand so aloof?
Not one day standing for reconciliation and truth?
America, judgement day is now at hand.
There is no escaping the Creator's true plan.
America's pathology must be openly revealed.
That is the only way we can naturally be healed.
So, I council you to hear my appeal and the Creators word will set the seal.
It is time for the truth and reconciliation,
It is time to own up to your human abomination.
It is time to make this wrong, a right.

The Healing of the African American Soul
*It is time to turn on the emancipation of light. Not
light that is colored in black or in white.
But light that can liberate us from this plight.
The truth is designed to set us free,
Only then we can be like
One family,
In the Creator's model human community.*

Wali Sabir
2/6/2013

The Healing of the African American Soul

Chapter 3: Hemorrhaging of Social Intelligence

"Strong people don't put others down... they lift them up"
Michael P. Watson

In the unfolding drama of the American experiment that is being played out over this 400-year journey, some major players have been staged, and we need to be clear about who they are and the role they play in our lives.

First, we have the indigenous people who are being infringed upon, including people of African origin, some of whom were already here in the Americas before the advent of the transatlantic slave trade. Then, you have the European immigrant, which comprises a wide range of people coming to this new land for many different reasons. In this number are the many banished criminals exported from European jails to the "New World."

I doubt if any of them came because they had experienced enough of the good life they were living in Europe and simply wanted a change. Then you have distinctly from amongst the Europeans, what I refer to as those profiteers: the marketeers, the exploiters, the slave makers, the materialists, and the social manipulators, interchangeably. These are the ones who consciously decided to engage the unwitting "stars" of this social drama: the enslaved African people of color.

The Healing of the African American Soul

We have already talked at length about the makeup of early colonial society, "pre" the social uprising called *The Bakers Rebellion*. The main point in that discussion is that the social manipulators knew that the social structure of the society had to be changed from one that disadvantaged them numerically to one where they had the advantage in numbers. The act in this major scene was to be accomplished by co-opting the mass population of European immigrants into a common social definition.

The slave makers (social manipulators) understood that the likeness of words makes people into a particular image. So, they had to create a word environment or word culture that justified, supported, and encouraged their chosen course of action. They had to make their scheme seem totally in agreement with the natural process of life. I want to submit as evidence the English Dictionary as clear and living proof of their strategy. Just look at their treatment of the terms "black and white" in their dictionary.

There are more than 130 synonyms, explanations, or definitions for the word black; none of them are positive. They range from dirty, wicked, death, evil, dismal, all the way to people of dark skin. On the other hand, White has more than 120 synonyms, explanations, or definitions, all of which are positive. Ranging from words like good, angelic, pure, and innocent, all the way to people with white skin and even defined as god-like. They did not stop there; they even linked their scheme to nature by implying that black is of the night, where bad things happen. Never mind all the good stuff that happens at night, nor the terrible crimes committed in the "whiteness" of daylight.

They put their religious and scientific scholars to work to devise and create pseudo-proof that justified their subhuman assertions. We have made the point that these

The Healing of the African American Soul

were actions of people who controlled the levers of power and social authority more than once. Scripture asks us an important question, and it says: "would a man rob G-d?" Then, the scripture answers its own question, "yes, even of a whole people." Who is this man or mind in the earth that feels daring enough to rob The Creator? And how did he go about doing it? In the role of the mental or rational makeup, there is a part of our natural development that can be referred to as the *Jinn*.

The Jinn, further defined, is an aspect of human nature and development. In its extreme state, it is highly rational, with little tolerance for the balanced, natural, progressive process of moving from lower to higher development, from weakness into strength. Because of its impatience and unbridled passions and appetite, it seeks to intervene against the natural process with a hasty scheme of its own, disrespectful, unnatural, and extreme. According to its own fanatical logic, it believes it is doing the work serving its own misguided idea of The Creator's Plan.

In Eastern philosophy, the Jinn as an aspect of human nature is neither inherently good nor bad. Its purpose is to serve the ambition of the human being however one chooses or is driven to engage it, according to their own free will and freedom of choice. The Last Prophet, upon him be prayers and peace, said that "we all, as human beings, have a Jinn expression in our nature; I have subdued mine" he said, "to be one that submits to The Will of G-d." Therefore, an unchecked Jinn nature can wreak havoc, mayhem, and corruption in the individual's life and to the people in an entire community or society.

The Healing of the African American Soul

The social manipulators (slave makers) allowed their own Jinn nature to take them down a path that had no faith in The Creator's Plan for human life according to the nature of His creation itself. They saw evolving human beings in their own cultural right, perhaps viewed in developmental, unrefined, and unfinished states of being through the European lens. And the Cold European Northerners judged them according to his European criteria, not knowing or considering Hot African Southerner criteria. And through their narrow vision, they publicly proclaimed that the African people in their European assessment were naturally unfit for the honorable role that The Creator had created human beings for.

They took the position that "we will prove to The Creator their unworthiness." According to European Church Theology, they knew their own creation as being no more than a word, and the word is understood to be a spiritual entity that can manifest in physical form.

These Jinn knew that The Creator said, "In the beginning was the word and the word was The Creator and with The Creator." So, to prove their plan, they knew that they could not *create* the word, but they could *corrupt* it. Could a man rob G-d? Yes, even of a whole people. When an accomplished thief steals something from you, you usually do not know it is gone until you need it. Sometimes they leave the container it was housed in but take the content. The thief that robbed G-d took the human content but preserved the physical container.

To accomplish this, they had to rig the system, which is what slave culture is. **Rigged** is described as **something** set in the proper order for optimal utility and usage or is **fixed in a dishonest, concocted, or unnatural way** to guarantee the desired outcome. A boat prepared for

The Healing of the African American Soul

readiness to sail can be an example of a rigged boat. A contest where the winner is predetermined beforehand is an example of a competition that is rigged. In slave culture, most people can agree that the system is rigged to benefit so-called white people as the predetermined winner.

However, as is evident in today's reality, they were not indeed winners, not in the long run, nor balanced morally in human development. The current political climate is divided into extreme camps; people on both sides of the political divide claim truthfully that the corrupted system is undoubtedly rigged.

People on both sides are right; indeed, the system is rigged. However, while they point at each other as being the blame for societal problems, the real enemy eludes them both. But justice is at hand. The only predetermined winner is the true enemy of the human being. The one that set up the system in the first place has been the only *temporal* winner.

The main objective of this "*time-restricted loser*" is to prove the human being unworthy of the Creator's gift to the human being as the manager and the custodial caretaker of the creation. That enemy, the one we have been known to call the devil or the Satan, but in reality, it is a mindset of arrogance, pride, and disregardfulness that has no faith in the nobility of the human constitution state of being. That mindset can take up residence in any human being that gives him or herself over to lies, falsehood, and weak ideas instead of the will to stand up for truth and be upright.

Much of the conflict in human society exists because we do not adequately understand our true enemy. All so-called "religions" have some philosophical approach or perspective to help us visualize and contend with evil's seen and unseen forces. However, to the degree that the adult masses are treated in the likeness of kindergarten or developmentally disabled children, where they are conditioned to only relate to a concrete world, their human development is arrested in the concept of a material god and in a material devil.

Any idea, concept, or philosophy that does not free the human mind from moving from weakness to strength or from immaturity to maturity is a form of oppression. The author of oppression is the mind that sees itself as *better* or *superior* to the true human being in its human essence. That **obsessed Jinn mind expressed** in its extreme form is the embodiment of what is referred to as the Devil or the Satan or the Deceiver or the Snake or the Serpent, often manifested in a personified image or caricature.

How do we contend with the devil or Satan? We have been given great council by a profound teacher and scholar of human salvation, designated America's Imam Warith-Deen Mohammed. He said, "We should not try to fight the devil or Satan head-on; he is too elusive (in his nature) for that." He said, "The only way to fight him is to identify his schemes and to fight the schemes." Whiteness is the number one scheme of the enemy of the human being today.

Whiteness is the elephant in the room. So that we can ensure being on the same page, let me state what I mean by "the elephant in the room." Whiteness is a thing in our lives that looms bigger than life. Whiteness sets the stage for our measurements in life. Whiteness sets the standard for what we see as beauty and non-beauty. Whiteness sets the mark for what is success and what is failure. Whiteness also

The Healing of the African American Soul manifests as an emotional state that everyone wants in their lives, in one way or another, consciously or subconsciously.

Whiteness has even been established as a standard, yardstick, and benchmark for all right, moral, exemplary, and G-d like. This dire scheme allowed the evil slave makers to accomplish so many objectives, necessarily established, to achieve their goal. As we have already pointed out, Whiteness is a colonial invention created from an emotional need for materialistic greed and ignorant fear.

Simply stated, the North American masses that made up the workforce were from Europe and Africa. These groups found that they had more in common than not. They were all being exploited by the ruling elite, which the masses significantly outnumbered. Like all human beings with common needs and interests, they can work together in an organized way to bring about change.

This represented a great challenge and a potential threat to the ruling elite. Divide and conquer was their answer. No stone was left unturned in bringing about this division. First, they had to make sure that there was a physical separation and, most importantly, a mental or psychological break. To bring about the physical separation, they passed laws preventing the union of so-called white people and so-called black people. They passed environmental laws that put so-called black people in a perpetual atmosphere of slave status. They simultaneously passed laws granting certain privileges and elevated social status to so-called white people. Note: These are the steps that mark the beginning of white privilege.

They violated the second commandment to bring about the mental separation, "thou shalt not make unto

The Healing of the African American Soul

thee any graven images." They defiantly formed and presented god in the image of whiteness. The superiority of whiteness was established as the lifeblood of slave culture, and it worked against the natural common needs, desires, and interests of all human beings. Whiteness took G-d out of the realm of spirituality and made him physical.

The system was rigged with the illusion of whiteness, associated with pigmentation, as the predetermined winner. In other words, So-called White people have been materialized to the degree that they see physical skin color as the most determinate factor of their human worth and present them explicitly as the natural winners in the human "race."

I use the term race here to point to the struggle among different social and cultural groups to strive, thrive, and gain more resources of nature that they saw as scarce. This is a crucial point to understand in the fabrication of whiteness as a social construct. This is the case because, as the Europeans discovered the "new world," poverty and destitution were an ever-present reality of European life.

Their social systems and the institutions that made them up were minimal, unenlightened and ill-conceived, and bred destitution. Ignorance, corruption, social disparity, and consequently, warring, discord, mayhem, and in-fighting were the order of the day. Nothing about European life would give you the idea that there was something special about having pale or so-called white skin. So, whiteness as an identity and much less as a sense of worthiness did not even exist.

Whiteness, as an arrangement, came to be established as the gold standard that determined how all people should see the world. It shaped the lens from which

The Healing of the African American Soul

we envisioned our perspectives and world view. Our worldview is defined by images and words that shape our thinking. The words that shape our thinking are determined by the one that taught us how to SPELL. As we stated earlier, words do make people. We should note that it is no mere coincidence that spelling or giving meaning, definition, and legal standards to the English language and the legal dehumanization of the enslaved people, were in fact, happening at the same time.

The mere fact that as human beings, we would willingly identify ourselves as whites and blacks are evidence that we are under a SPELL. What is a spell? A spell is an emotional state where you operate under the control or sway of someone else. In other words, you are not in possession of your own mind. For human beings, the mind is the faculty by which they think, conceive, perceive, feel, remember, or desire.

It is also the instrument through which they logically reconcile the material reality with the nonmaterial reality. The spell of whiteness makes one blind to the non-material reality. Material things are finite and concrete; they have a beginning and an end; they are a part of a tangible closed system. The enemy of the human being wants the human being to have a closed mind, a small mind, a concrete, limited material-centered mind, while the mind, in actuality, is virtual and logical.

When one is under the control or the sway of someone else, their own thinking, perception, feelings, and total awareness of self and others are altered. They are not grounded in their own authentic reality. That is the current state of our public. Today, truth is understood relative to

The Healing of the African American Soul

one's emotional state, which is influenced by personal inclinations, likes, and desires.

When one's likes and desires have been materialized, one cannot operate in their true, higher state of human being. When one is in such a state, they are subject to confuse morality with moralism. Morality is having the discernment between right and wrong. Moralism being, the need to be right at any cost, even when you are wrong. Moralism gives itself to making others unsuitable by lying to yourself.

In their true reality, the human being is spiritual beings with a physical or material body to express their spiritual life. When the spiritual life is suppressed, the material-centered life can only be used as a tool governed by "drives" and taken down any path that suits the directives of the social manipulators. Such people become indiscriminate consumers of alternative facts.

They become the unwitting defenders of these alternative facts in the face of evidence to the contrary because these alternative facts have become their life and embedded in their lifestyles. They are vested in their material form at the expense of their own moral sanity. The price is paid in all their emotional, intellectual, spiritual, and physical well-being. Whiteness is indeed a WMD, a Weapon of Mass Destruction where the outcome is MAD, Mutual Assured Destruction.

Human society evolves in stages, when we, as human beings, see and comprehend our common interests and common needs and then socially address them. This is the bedrock of human progress, as it manifests in societal life. Nature says there are enough resources to meet all needs with the right moral intent and mental cultivation and

The Healing of the African American Soul
motivation to take action. Only a narrow and self-centered interest blinds us of this reality.

This is the case with the establishment of whiteness as a social construct. The human family has been derailed from the natural pattern of human growth and development. The measuring stick of universal truth and laws have become second rate to alternative facts, hoaxes, falsehoods, and fake news. The voice of the caller, calling to truth, justice, and upright living, can barely be heard in such an environment.

Whiteness indeed has inflicted a devastating wound on the ex-slave people of America, but as we pointed out before, whiteness is a WMD, a Weapon of Mass Destruction that has been shot in the heart of sociability of all people. Whiteness has the social intelligence of the whole world hemorrhaging with no real sense of how to stop the bleeding.

Dr. Brad Blanton, Ph.D., points out in his book "Radical Honesty" that a significant cause of so much sickness both biologically and emotionally is "lying." He points out how in his practice, honesty has resolved many emotional and physical illnesses. If we are to get to the heart of our collective problem, whiteness is the number one scheme of the enemy of the human being that must be dealt with. To properly heal this world, it can no longer be ignored! We all need truth and reconciliation!

The Healing of the African American Soul
The Elephant in the Room

America the beautiful.
America the beast.
From which of the tables are you able to feast?
All men are created equal.
And not denied their human right, Or reduced to beast of the field. cut off from all avenues of seeing the light?
America the beautiful.
America the beast.
From which of the tables are you able to feast?
The table spread of universal law.
Or the serpents brew of Satan's claw?
The latter more than any is what has prevailed,
America's beauty descending to a hell is entailed.
Morality uprooted by self-righteous moralism,
Human nature turned upside down by our enemy's wrong prism.
Through the eyes of whiteness is the all-consuming world view,
Where men are judged on skin color and not what they do.
America the beautiful.
America the beast.
From which of the tables are you able to feast?
Whiteness is the big elephant occupying the room,
Never spoken, its awe and power we just come to assume.
Whiteness consumes all that succumbs to her embrace,
It kills the spirit and objectifies the whole human race.
Men blind to their commonality and interdependence,
Making their destruction all but an assured refringence.

The Healing of the African American Soul

America the beautiful.
America the beast.
From which of the tables are you able to feast?
To avoid a pending, unavoidable doom,
We must come together to expose this elephant in the room!

Wali Sabir
12/30/19

The Healing of the African American Soul

Chapter 4: The Cascade of Healing in Reverse

That which is inhuman cannot be divine.
Frederick Douglass

The slave went free, stood a brief moment in the sun, then went back toward slavery.
W.E.B. Du Bois, Black Reconstruction in America

"**Black Lives Matter**." There are two main descriptions of matter we want to consider here: physical substance in general, as distinct from mind and spirit; (in physics) that occupies space and possesses rest mass, especially as distinct from energy. Another is to be of importance, to have significance. Undoubtedly, the latter meaning is the one implied in the now popular slogan, "Black Lives Matter."

However, here is the problem: the former consideration is the cultural and historical meaning of black. Physical substance, in general, as distinct from mind and spirit. Also, when you add the *shade* that the English language gives to *black* in the form of adjectives that clearly painted the picture and intent of black as a social construct, you do not come away seeing black as of any importance or having any significance. On the surface, the outcry that "Black Lives Matter" is a strong emotional appeal, but when you peel back its layers, a poisonous pill is exposed.

The poison pill is the spell cast by the inherent meaning in the language of slave culture: black and white.

The Healing of the African American Soul

"Just watching the Republican Convention ... they are spewing this fear, like all you hear is Donald Trump ... and all of them talking about fear – we are the ones being killed, we are the ones getting shot, we are the ones being denied to live in certain communities, or we've been hanged, we been shot and all you keep hearing about – fear – it's amazing – why we keep loving this country, and this country does not love us back."

These are passionate words made by Doc Rivers, a well-respected NBA coach, as he fought to hold back the tears. The reality is that the ruling elite declared war on the people of African descent in the late 1600s. This was done when they knew that as a matter of their survival, they had to distort and redefine reality and create an oppressive word environment to restructure colonial society.

They gave birth to whiteness as a label for people with pale, unpigmented skin like themselves, as a means of distinction from other ordinary non-pale skinned, melanin people. The fear that they were spurring at the Republican Convention in 2020 was the same fear that the elite of colonial society in the late 1600s had. They feared that the common mass of human beings would unite around their humanity, concern for their fellow human beings, and rise up against the oppressive tyranny.

Yes, war was declared and has been waged on enslaved and the formerly enslaved people since the founding period of this country. So, Coach Doc Rivers' statement was right on point, "it's amazing- why we keep loving this country and this country does not love us back." Love is a human characteristic in opposition to fear. Their fear of us won't let them see us as human beings deserving

The Healing of the African American Soul

of love. It is cognitive dissonance at work that compels them to see us as less than human outwardly.

War, according to Wikipedia, is an intense armed conflict between states, governments, societies, or paramilitary groups such as mercenaries, insurgents, and militias. It is generally characterized by extreme violence, aggression, destruction, deception, and mortality, using regular or irregular military forces.

Warfare refers to the common activities and characteristics of types of war or of wars in general. Total war is not restricted to purely legitimate military targets and can result in massive civilian or other non-combatant suffering and casualties. We must be clear that "total war" was waged on us, the formerly enslaved people, from founding these United States of America. So again, it's amazing – how do we keep loving this country and this country does not love us back.

We have talked about what happens under natural circumstances when the physical body is wounded in the cascade of healing. We know the first and most immediate step is to stop the bleeding, cleanse the wound and kill the bacteria, rebuild the wounded area with healthy material, and mature the new material toward full recovery and strength. The total war that was waged on the enslaved and formerly enslaved people was and is to ensure that none of these natural processes kick in.

In fact, it is engrained in official U.S. policy to reverse the natural order of things affecting the formerly enslaved people's lives. U.S. official policy of total war against the African descendants is clearly laid out in records of the late 1600s and throughout the 1700s and 1800s. However, the

The Healing of the African American Soul

most vivid expression of this total war can be seen in what came to be known as the *Jim Crow Era*.

In her New York Times Bestseller, "The New Jim Crow," Michelle Alexander paints a clear picture of this time, the climate, and the prevailing attitudes about how the formerly enslaved people are treated. The fear that Doc Rivers observed coming from the mouth of those who label themselves as conservatives is the same fear that gave rise to the reign of terror under the label of Jim Crow. It is noted that current stereotypes of so-called black men as angry, aggressive, vengeful, unruly predators can be traced to this period when the so-called whites feared that an angry mass of so-called vindictive black men might rise up and counterattack them or counter-rape their women.

She also points out similar facts as did Shaw Rochester. In his book "Black Tax," both of them make the case that Jim Crow was a time period right after the civil war when the southern economy was totally destroyed, and cotton trade ran the global economy. The loss of free slave labor, which the economy was built on, harmed the southern economy in particular and the global economy in general. Jim Crow was about getting what would be, in effect, "free labor" back out of the newly freed people.

Every instrument of society was used to ensure the language of black and white be engaged to embed fear as an automatic reaction to all social interaction between the two ethnic and de facto cultural groups. "Fear" for the so-called white people was based on their concerns that the enslaved and formerly enslaved people would do to the so-called white people what had been and what was being done to them. "Fear" for the so-called black people was their rightful concern for their lives, to the extent that they dare

The Healing of the African American Soul

not violate the infraction of established social norms of white supremacy, consciously or even unconsciously.

During this period, those subject to committing these social violations included the many aspiring ex-slaves with high hopes of becoming free and self-sufficient.

There are many stories of schools that were opened to educate themselves, and farms purchased to feed themselves, institutions and businesses designed to support themselves and support others, and even homes built to house themselves. We know that they were outright attacked, lynchings took place, castrations, live burnings, homes burnt to the ground, men, women, and children ran off of their own land by homegrown terrorists dressed in "white" sheets and "white" masks.

Jim Crow was a government-supported, institutionalized all-out war on the ex-slaves; we experienced 100 years of lynching, sharecropping, and convict leasing as new organized and more sophisticated forms of slavery. We saw the birth of the Ku Klux Klan (KKK) and an undeniable reign of terror that lives on, even until this current day. Every institution in the society worked systemically to deepen the wounds of the ex-slave people at that time.

Whereas the natural principles in the *cascade of healing* addressed our physical wounds, the similar principles to meet our social wounds' needs were completely shut down. The reality of Jim Crow deepened the soul-based wounds of our social sensibilities and social sensitivities. Jim Crow, by far, was worse than physical slavery because the enforcement of whiteness took on a penetrating new meaning.

The Healing of the African American Soul

It was effective to the point where so-called black inferiority and human denigration, as defined by the slave culture, began to be internalized and imbibed en masse by the formerly enslaved people themselves. We were rigged to feel ashamed of simply being born. We were conditioned to be victims of shame perpetually. They did not want us to feel any dignity about living our own human lives.

This internalization and re-institutionalization of slavery through whiteness is the *cascade of social healing* in reverse. To comprehend this, let's re-visit and take another look at the natural process in the *cascade of healing*. First, healing is a process that works to make whole again or to make healthy again. For the formerly enslaved people, to "make whole or well again" can be likened, if you will, to the statement to "make America Great Again." For us, the formerly enslaved people, America has never been great for our lives.

Perhaps it felt great for those at war with us, as our enemies live under whiteness's ruling classification. But yes, there is a promise of her greatness as a contingency. That contingency is: if she lives up to her own creed of men being created equal with certain inalienable rights, including life, liberty, and the pursuit of happiness. However, the reality is that America has enacted every measure conceivable to make sure that the formerly enslaved population never realized that promise of life, liberty, and the pursuit of happiness.

In the case of a physical wound, an overlapping four-phase process kicks in. The components are hemostasis, defensive, proliferative, and maturation. The first phase is stopping the bleeding. The next phase is focused on killing the bacteria and cleaning the wound. Thirdly, the focus is

The Healing of the African American Soul

on filling and covering the wound. The fourth and final phase of focus is on the new tissue slowly gaining strength and flexibility. Here, collagen fibers reorganize, the tissue remodels and matures, and there is an overall increase in tensile strength on the way to full recovery.

In the case of social or psychological wounds, the language of slave culture, black and white, deepens the wound and causes perfused hammering and agitation. The bacteria of lies fester and spread to break down our defenses and our internal and external supportive relationships with ourselves and others. These lies cut us off from seeing our own reality and any inherent value we have as unique creatures of The Creator. The ability to use a sense of self-worth is cut off and arrested in a state of relapsing immaturity.

To understand the *cascade of social healing,* we must understand what social blood is in proper context. The social blood of the human being is common sense. Senses are the faculties through which we perceive and process external stimuli to reconcile our external reality with our internal reality in our minds. Without this mental balance, we are like fish out of water.

Common sense is described as sound judgment in practical matters. Common sense then is fundamental or rudimentary knowledge that allows a person or group of people to be grounded in their own practical reality. It is said that the acid test for any living organism is its ability to adjust and adapt to its environment. This means having the ability to make sound judgment, given the situation in the "here and now."

Therefore, when there is a social wound, the bleeding is the inability of the person or group of people to stop the

The Healing of the African American Soul

bleeding by using their common sense to make the necessary adjustments or adaptations in their environment, to maintain and thrive productively, in this case, to stop the bleeding. Their common sense is rendered to be not so common.

Their sense perception is skewed in a way that does not work for their own benefit. The components that make up the social blood are dormant and passive. Their sense of educational, economic, governmental, and cultural awareness is built on a foundation of lies. The lies of whiteness!

The first step of self-awareness, to be grounded in one's own reality, is missing, and the ability to stop the bleeding is not working effectively for our own good. Then, the contamination of our sociability moves towards regression in the contaminated filth of a corrupt word environment, where low and unhealthy frequencies make it impossible for natural healing to occur. The result is our social intelligence becomes arrested, digressive and emotional, exacting social maturity to be unachievable.

Let me be clear on what I mean by "grounded in our own reality." Our senses are designed to keep us aware of what is happening in the context of the moment. Our senses are designed to work together, as an integrated community within the individual self, to decode incoming language, verbal or nonverbal, and other stimuli for the purpose of discernment and judgment.

When our senses function as they should through accurate sense perception, we are grounded in capturing our own reality. This grounding is subject to a dynamic process that allows us to be present in the state of the

The Healing of the African American Soul

moment. Being present in the moment will enable us to see things as they are, not based on what we want them to be.

Whiteness is set up or structured in our minds on the denial of true reality. Whiteness is truly a lie. I applaud the work of Dr. Robin DeAngelo, as she is devoted to her work to help so-called white people get grounded in their reality as being unavoidably racists. I agree with her; our work today is not about blaming or shaming. I want to take one step further by adding that whiteness as a lethal weapon of mass destruction will remain in place, wounding human beings at every social turn until we are prepared to reconstruct our word environment. The *cascade of social healing* will not kick-in, to stop the bleeding.

The social bird of education for the formerly enslaved people is grounded in someone else's false reality. Our educational institutions, schools, churches, temples, masjid or mosques, or any other means through which we receive motivating instructions, have not equipped us to be responsive to our needs as individuals and as a balanced, vibrant community.

The few examples of thoughtful responses to the oppressive nature of the system of whiteness are not enough. Any relative progress is dwarfed by the overwhelming reactionary nature of dealing with the total war on us at every level of social infrastructure construction.

We lead the world in high rates of morbidity and mortality because our "learned scholars" have not produced healthy protocols, formulations, and work directives designed to educate our public on the dangers of the lacking, un-wholistic *slave diet* that we grew to embrace culturally out of necessity. The slave diet, as pointed out

The Healing of the African American Soul

already, is a 3/5's diet designed to reverse the natural healing process. Our physical diet of high concentration of protein, carbohydrates, and fats is a metaphor for our materialized mental and spiritual diet deficits.

This is the reason why the more that we accessed education or miseducation in the 60's onward, the more we lost our moral high ground that our forebearers stood upon. With fewer means, they brought land, owned businesses, and prided themselves as being "race men and women"; that is, their actions were that which represented the best in our human character as formerly enslaved Americans of African descent.

With our more disposable material resources today, we are losing what they worked so hard to acquire with their blood, sweat, tears, and sacrifices. And even more so, we as a group have no sense of group pride and dignity any longer. Many of our permeating cultural expressions do not even possess the values of the lowest reptilian animal. Some of our self-denigrating group behavior would shame anybody among civilized men and women, claiming to be associating members of the human family.

The social bird of economics is the barometer of how fast we are moving in the wrong direction. The human being needs work, and especially the male human being needs work to feel his aliveness. Under the system of slavery, we had 100% employment because our labor was free. Under Jim Crow, there was nearly 100% employment as well. In many cases, the net result was that we paid for the share cropping system through rigged bookkeeping, free labor through convict leasing, and gross underpayment in all other forms of labor engagement.

The Healing of the African American Soul

With advances in technology, the need for manual workers grew less and less, and that common saying for the formerly enslaved people proved true, over and over, again, we were "the last hired and the first fired." Men that were accustomed to working all the time found themselves with no work, with a growing sense of hopelessness, worthlessness, and despair. Here again, we have no control over what is done to us by this system, but we do have control over how we either respond or react to what is done to us.

What we have been conditioned to do is to react. Our reaction is a part of the playbook of the social manipulators. The fact that we do not have a network of farmers growing food that we systematically support through a network of consumers that we organize throughout our communities is a gross example of our reactionary posture.

The fact is that that old adage of "I ain't gonna make that n*gg*r rich!" is very much a part of our prevailing psychological realism, more than likely, infused by the culture of white supremacy. In that rigged fermentation of self-hatred, we tend not to do business with one another. Integration American style is a reaction; it is the sub-group, the sub-culture that totally acquiesces to the dominating cultural group. Like, the formerly enslaved people giving up all their businesses to further enrich the enterprises of the dominant class, the dominant culture, the dominant influence.

Without proper education that is grounded in our own reality, we can have no realistic view to approach our own economic development. Without education and economic development, we have no political power to influence government policy related to us. Being powerless

The Healing of the African American Soul

and reactionary in these areas makes our cultural expressions also reactionary.

Our cultural expressions, to a large extent, are a self-fulfilling prophecy, it expresses what the social manipulators have invoked out of us and then write and say about us. The language in much of our cultural expressions is of low frequency, promoting poor health and negative thinking. Thinking that makes it impossible for us to unite around common causes, common needs, and common concerns.

The truth is that sociological war has been waged on us, and as Coach Doc Rivers said, "it's amazing – that we keep loving this country and this country don't love us back." Let's be clear, the U.S. government declared war on us at its very founding and has been unrelenting in its affront of us ever since.

Every effort as an attempt to provide some measure of redress for our unjust treatment, through unsustainable government policy and short-lived programs, they found ways to get around these efforts or rolling them back or withdrawing support. We need truth and reconciliation in order to stop the bleeding effectively. We need the truth to cleanse the wound and kill the bacteria. We need the truth to reach the hearts and sincere minds of stand-up right-minded human beings so that we truly begin the repair and the regeneration of our social wounds.

"If there is no struggle, there is no progress. Those who profess to favor freedom, and yet depreciate agitation, are men who want crops without plowing up the ground. They want rain without thunder and lightning. They want the ocean without the awful roar of its many waters. This

The Healing of the African American Soul

struggle may be a moral one, or it may be a physical one, or it may be both moral and physical, but it must be a struggle. Power concedes nothing without a demand. It never did, and it never will."

Frederick Douglass

"I have observed this in my experience of slavery - that whenever my condition was improved, instead of it increasing my contentment, it only increased my desire to be free and set me to thinking of plans to gain my freedom. To make a contented slave, I have found that it is necessary to make a thoughtless one. It is necessary to darken his moral and mental vision, and, as far as possible, to annihilate the power of reason. He must be able to detect no inconsistencies in slavery; he must be made to feel that slavery is right; and he can be brought to that only when he ceases to be a man." Frederick Douglass

The Healing of the African American Soul
We got to get it right

Family, we got to get it right!
We got to! – It's time now, we got to get out of this dark and step into the light!
I know hell, we know hell and hell is when you're not free.
Hell is when I may have – but not one thing comes from me.
My food, my clothes, my house and even the books I read,
They're thrown to me like hogs that masters feed.
Even the words I think and the words I used,
They have me rejecting myself and acting confused.
Buying hair and bleaching cream,
Spending money on reams and all kinds of trinkets and things.
What we are trying to buy, money will never acquire.
Which is someone else's reality and it's based on a lie.
Black get back, brown stick around, white come on down!
A society that can think no deeper than skin?
Tell me what race can such a people compete and still win?
We got to – it's time to get it right!
We got to get out of the dark and step into the light!
The worst crime is not the physical terror we take, and we took.
The worst crime is the arrested development and enslaved minds we have on the hook. More of our men in jail than were on the slave plantation,

The Healing of the African American Soul

And we remain in the dark to their scheming manipulation.

So, let's be clear on who is the real perpetrator of terror and injustice in our nation,
It is simply, without doubt, a clear case of human relation.
It's no mystery that some of them wear a white hooded sheet,
While some others wear badges, guns and steel toe boots on their feet.
But it is you and I that is profiled and marginalized,
So that in our victimhood our strength cannot be harnessed and capitalized.
My dear people, we got to get it right!
Beat back the darkness and establish the light!
We did it before and we can do it again, We have it from deep, deep inside, from with-in.
On black wall street the dollar turned 40 times before it left our community,
Family, businesses and institutions were the hallmark of our unity.
The way out of darkness, can't you see?
We had abundant love, respect and human dignity.
My dear people, we got to get it right!
We got to cast off the dark and stand in the light!
It does not take rocket science to change our condition,
We simply need to rethink our position.
Our priorities are clearly out of place, When we put first things first, we achieve amazing grace.
Our idea of religion has got to change, It is not our Creator that's making us insane.

The Healing of the African American Soul

When you are in the ditch and you cannot push in one direction to get free,
I say your mind is locked in mental slavery.

We declare we love our Creator, but we cannot work together for what is right,
Then we must question from what source are we seeking the light.
Dear people, it's time we get it right!
We got to get out of this dark and standup and fight!
Fight to stand in our own precious reality.
Doing for self is never another's' responsibility.
Common sense – that is truly what we need.
Turn the soil, plant the seed and pull out the weed. Do this in our homes and all our institutions,
Do the work and it will establish the real solutions?
It's time to get it right!
It's time to do the work, I can see the light!
In the words of Henry Ford,
"coming together is a beginning, Keeping it together is progress,
Working together is success."

Wali Sabir

Chapter 5: The Cascade of Social Healing

America is false to the past, false to the present, and solemnly binds herself to be false to the future.
Frederick Douglass

As stated above, the blood of our social life is our common sense. It flows through our individual and group life as principles and values that anchor us in our own reality. These principles and values allow us to accept things as they are, based on what is. These principles and values are dynamic and not static; they are grounded in universal laws that allow us to adjust based on time and conditions present in the moment. Common sense kicks in to stop the bleeding when lies come to injure our social intelligence. The lie of whiteness has wounded our social intelligence and, through the institution of slavery that has conditioned us to deny our reality.

So, suppose we are alive in our senses. In that case, it stands to reason that in our social blood of common sense, there is knowledge in our educational, economic, governmental, and cultural concerns that is available to stop the bleeding. Being alive in our senses means we can see, hear and feel what life and our environmental circumstances demand of us to move from a position of weakness toward a position of sustainable strength.

The Healing of the African American Soul

Next, to kill the bacteria of lies and cleans the wound, we must face our weaknesses and strengths and purify our actions and thoughts with a renewed commitment to a moral imperative. The next step is to be proactive to fill the wounded area with new truth, based on productive actions, and grounded in common sense (sound judgment) that is in the best interest of the individual and the community. Then we must expand our network to replicate goodness based on sound principles and values that benefit all.

Quran 13:11

For each one are successive [angels] before and behind him who protect him by the decree of The Creator. Indeed, He will not change the condition of a people until they change what is in themselves. And when The Creator intends for a people ill, there is no repelling it. And there is not for them besides Him any patron.

The Creator says to us that our condition will not change until we change what is troubling us. What is troubling our souls are the lies that shape our social interaction with ourselves and others. You cannot grow up in this society without lies being a significant part of what has shaped you. I want to share with you some aspects of my life, as I believe my life and what has shaped me, in many respects, is typical of how "whiteness" has shaped many former enslaved people. This is only a part of my story; I hope you can find it meaningful as I relate to you transparently, sharing my strengths and weaknesses.

My legal name is Waliyyuddin Abdul Sabir; I was born with the name Dossie Lee Harris. I changed the spelling of my first name to Dorsey because I was named after my paternal uncle, and that is the way he spelled his first name. I was born July 29, 1945, to Mossett and Vallie

The Healing of the African American Soul

Harris of Durham, North Carolina. I was born the 5th child of 9. My parents were not what you might call very educated, my father went to the 4th grade, and my mother went to the 11th grade. Both my parents were religious people. My father was of the Primitive Baptist faith, and my mother was Baptist. All my siblings and I attended my mother's church, and I can't say we consciously chose my mother's brand of Christianity over my father's.

As a dark-skinned, unaware of self, male child, growing up in the '50s and '60s was not easy, by any stretch of the imagination. As I look back at those times, I marble at my mother and father's ingenuity to feed eight growing boys and one girl. We did not have a lot or the best quality food at times, but we did not starve. Even though I sometimes recall eating what we called air bread sandwiches, two pieces of white bread with nothing between them.

The clothes I got were mostly hand-me-downs from my older brothers if they had any life left in them. The house I grew up in was small for eleven people. We had no running water, no indoor bathroom, nor central heat for most of the time I was at home. We got the air conditioning from the cold draft in the winter and the heat in the summer. Winters were incredibly challenging as we had to crowd around the pot-belly stove to get some measure of warmth.

In my preschool years, I do not remember much, but I do know I was not prepared to enter a structured learning environment with other children who had been equipped with some fundamentals of the three "R's." I started school in the first grade when I was six years old but was not promoted to the 2nd grade the following year. I was very

The Healing of the African American Soul

slow in learning to read and developed a complex about my poor reading abilities. I developed no genuine interest other than the typical childhood likes and dislikes. I like playing what we thought were fun games, like rolling tires and cowboys and Indians. Like most oppressed people, they are programmed to root for the oppressor.

My self-image was very poor as I consider myself to be non-attractive, with undesirable dark skin, and definitely not smart. I was very reserved outside of my limited social group of friends. Even though I did not read well, I was a deep thinker. My third-grade teacher told me, boy, if you could read, you would be brilliant. I had a breakthrough in the 7th or 8th grade, and I had a teacher, Mr. Owen Coward, who was my math teacher. He taught me math in a way that increased my confidence and allowed me to become a good math student. Even though I still struggled with the other subjects, I became good in this area.

Though I grew up with loving parents, I never received any guidance on preparing to be a man. I was never told how to keep going after what I perceived as a failure, so my past is littered with one failed attempt after another. I was shy and introverted and saw no example that I could relate to in my environment on how to communicate. I knew my parents worked hard and struggled to make ends meet, and had conflicts over money issues from time to time. I grew up with no sense of money, and I did not know how to make it or keep it. I learned how to work but knew nothing about money and money management.

While in high school, I, along with my brothers, was very involved in the civil rights movement. We participated

The Healing of the African American Soul

in most, if not all, civil rights protest activities in Durham and the surrounding areas. While on the picket line, I recall being spit in my face and knife held to my throat by a big "white" boy. I was told later that he was a football player at Duke University.

This event led to an extensive, well-publicized trial in Durham; the next night, the same guy came back and confronted my brother, one older than me; let's say it was not nonviolent. The boy ended up in the hospital, and my brother was arrested. My brother was cleared of all charges at the trial. What stands out in my mind about that incident was the sense of powerlessness and fear that I had at that moment. The boldness and misplaced righteous indignation of his attack are what played over and over in my mind. As I came to have more insight, I looked back in wonderment, how is it that someone can take such a strong stand on perpetuating injustice on another human being?

I am a product of whiteness. Early in my life, whiteness conditioned me to have low exceptions and no imagination. I did not know to permit myself to think beyond the box of whiteness that I allowed to shape my reality. I saw myself as a good person but willing to go along with immorality because I thought this is what you have to do to make it. I knew nothing about true responsibility as a man, husband, and father figure, to protect and secure my family.

I grew up being unestablished in every dimension of my life. However, I have always been a seeker of truth. I have always wanted to know how things are naturally put together. Growing up with loving parents, seven brothers and one sister, we all reaching to do our best from the moral example set by our parents. Yet, we all wobbled under the

The Healing of the African American Soul

pressure of life because the static balance we got from church, school, and all of our social interactions were insufficient for authentic establishment in the human community.

In the case of static balance, we looked ok on the surface while nothing was being done. But engaging in the responsibilities of life is another matter. My confidence was so shallow I did not really apply myself to anything. I approached life from the back door; what I did was not based on any real intention nor preparation. After high school, I attended college for one semester. I felt totally out of place and made no attempt to do the required work to stay in school, and I was not confident I could do the work.

I left college and joined the U.S. Airforce in 1966. In retrospect, I see the same pattern unfolding in everything I attempted to do. While in the Airforce, I did have some small breakthroughs. I brought some basic English grammar books and worked to better my communication skills. As I began to understand more about English grammar, I began to put my thoughts on paper. I found writing to be very therapeutic in that it helped me organize my thoughts and have a clearer picture of what I was seeing around me.

The more I saw what was going on around me, the more contentious I became. In Florida, the Air Base I was on was typical of the south and its views on formally enslaved people. I protested in every way I knew how. I grew an afro hairstyle against regulation. I was so much of a rebel that I would staple my strips on so I would not have to unstitch them as I lost them.

One incident I was very vocal about is, my roommate was a hard worker; he knew his job and did it well.

The Healing of the African American Soul

However, instead of being promoted to a higher rank and job assignment, he trained a lower-ranking airman, who happened to be Caucasian. This airman of lower rank became his supervisor and was promoted to a higher rank than him. I earned the nickname "H-Rap" and was profiled as a troublemaker. Even though I got an honorable discharge, they told me I could not reenlist if I wanted to.

However, the most memorable experience that I had that best displayed the impact and profoundly ingrained nature of whiteness happened in a U.S. Airforce theater. Safety was a high priority, in that airmen getting into automobile accidents was not an uncommon thing. So, safety reviews were staged periodically. At one such event, I recall walking into a theater with what seems to be approximately 200 or more other airmen.

The safety film started with a young European American boy and girl driving at a high rate of speed and resulting in a fatal accident. They showed the police going to the victims' homes and sadly informing the parents of their loss. You could feel the emotion of sadness and empathy in the room. Next, the depiction was of two African American men traveling in an old, not attractive automobile. The one in the passenger seat was asleep, and the one driving was sleepy. They showed the driver falling asleep and running into the rear of the tractor-trailer. What was most despicable to me was upon impact; the whole theater audience erupted in laughter. I was upset with the entire thing, but I was disappointed that I did not see other African American Airmen with the same outrage that I had.

I was discharged from the Air Force in 1970. I received a three-month early out to return back to North Carolina Central University. I had taken some college

The Healing of the African American Soul

courses while in the service and felt better prepared on this go-round. However, I came back to school in an environment of protest and revolutionary rhetoric, which was more to my liking than school.

I became a part of a small group that wanted to train and prepare for the revolution. We studied the revolutionary tactics of other oppressed people and began to develop some strategies of our own. One of my strategies was taking a job with Operation Breakthrough as a youth organizer. This, I believed, would allow me to move about and identify other like-minded individuals that we could enroll in our cause. But the most unexpected thing happened in the course of my work. I was assigned to work with the local Temple of the Nation of Islam, Mosque number 34, in a joint effort to sponsor a business Bazaar.

This was a significant turning point when I met Minister Kenneth X Murray. Thou I had been exposed to the Nation of Islam before, while I was in service, his example as a leader and what he saw in me gave me some direction in my life. Here many of the unanswered questions I had about the revolution began to come into focus for me.

I wanted to know, once we start the armed struggle, how do we maintain it? How do we feed ourselves and maintain the necessities for ongoing engagement? How do we build a base of supporters for the cause? I saw no answers coming from our small circle of would-be revolutionaries. The Nation of Islam became my life. The doors would hardly swing at the Temple without my presence.

I became one of Minister Kenneth X's assistance ministers in a relatively short period of time. I wore all

The Healing of the African American Soul

kinds of hats, from baker to builder. I also became one of the founders of our private school, which we called the University of Islam. I worked as one of the teachers and Den of boys. This was indeed a transformational experience for me. To teach, I had to become a student and what I studied most was nature. That allowed me to relate to my students in ways that grounded us in our own reality.

For example, in math, we studied the language of math, how whole numbers and fractions are applied to our life. We talked about how to be a part of something; you have to be complete within yourself. I used whatever came up as a teaching lesson. For example, one of the boys told another boy that he had police car hair. I said, what kind of hair? He said hair that rolls up and stops anywhere. The whole class erupted in laughter. For a few days, all we talked about was hair. They did research papers on hair and gained tremendous respect for themselves and the true beauty of their own hair.

Through my work as Den of boys, my interest grew in a broader approach to education. I realized that the families I was working with and I had no fundamental knowledge of family life. It was confirmed to me that the dysfunction I saw in the children was a reflection of their family life. It was around this time that another major shift happened in my life. In 1975, Imam Mohammed became the leader of the Nation Of Islam (N.O.I.) after his father's death.

He came in talking about the natural process that we were created in and how that must be the foundation that our lives are built on. He said that words make people. He began to unravel the ladder we were climbing, leaning against the wall of false religious instruction while giving us

The Healing of the African American Soul

profound insight into the approach his father had taken to counter the schemes of the enemy to keep us engulfed in his trap of whiteness.

My main interest stemmed from my work with families, was to understand the social dynamics around our disempowerment and the nature of our dysfunction. I began to study the words that made my own family and read whatever I could about family development. I founded a nonprofit called Family Development Workshop. From that effort, I produced my first book, The Reconstruction of the African American Male. From that effort, the subsequent books, The Anatomy of Change and Liberating Minds from an Oppressive Word Environment, continue our honorable leader's vision and mission and establish model community life.

Another significant influence in my life was meeting and working with Carton Hargrove. Carton owned a company called Leadership Development Institute. The company's main focus was on transformational technology. It featured a thirty-hour intensive workshop called "Awareness and Awaking's." The motto of the workshop was "how you do anything is how you do everything."

This was transformative work. I trained as an associate instructor and gained valuable insight into social and human dynamics. The more insight I gained on how I did anything, the more I began to understand how I habitually did everything. I realized that to the degree that I was boxed in, it was due to the limitations I put on my own self.

The greatest takeaway for me from this training was the exploration of my why. It has been said, "if your why

The Healing of the African American Soul

don't make you cry, then it is not big enough." It is also noted that "if your why is big enough, the facts don't count." The main point is that "why" is one of the biggest motivators in life. With one's "why" being such a powerful force for motivation, on the flip side, there must be a powerful force when there is a total lack of motivation for doing something vitally important. Confronting this dilemma has been my life's work.

This dilemma can be seen in a story that is one of the main points in my writings. For me, it is quite a revealing experience. About a little more than thirty years ago, I was talking with my nephew. He said some things that troubled me. I wanted to express to him what I saw in what he was saying in a way that his seven-year-old mind could understand. I want you to picture this. I took a white sheet of paper; on one side, I drew a black dot. On the other, I had a white dot. I had about twenty words in the center of the page, like good, bad, ugly, wrong, right, G-d, devil, life, death, etc. I had a line to the right and left of each word under the black and white dots.

I asked him to check off how he saw the words under the appropriate dot for him. I said there are no right or wrong answers for you; just check what comes up for you. As you can imagine, he checked off under the black dot for every word that had a negative connotation. Every word with a positive connotation he checked off under the white dot. I then turned the paper over and with still a black dot and a white dot but on this side; I had one word "YOU." I asked him, so, what are you? He said Blk..., he did not say the whole word. He connected in his seven-year-old mind how he had been socialized to see black and did not like what he saw.

The Healing of the African American Soul

I went on to do the same exercise with about three hundred and fifty young men in the midnight basketball league in Hartford, CT, and got the same result practically. I have done it with many other individuals, and the results are no different. I have not been able to get any European Americans to do the exercise. So far, the ones that I have asked, they refuse once they see the exercise. The reaction is almost like Dracula being presented with a cross. Even after hearing this story, I challenge you to do the exercise for yourself. The emotion you go through is quite revealing. The Word Environment Exercise is at the end of this chapter for you.

In the process of trying to understand my "why," I was brought face to face with the reality and nature of the dysfunction that is so persistent in my personal life and the life of the ex-slave community as a whole. The point I make along with the exercise is that it is essential to understand that while slavery was being perfected as a social institution, the English language was simultaneously standardized. Therefore, it is no accident that all descriptions of black are negative and all for white are positive.

These descriptions of black and white are just as deliberate as poverty is for the so-called black and wealth is for the so-called white. Just as deliberate as injustice is for the so-called black and justice is for the so-called white. We need truth and reconciliation. This is not to say that all so-called white has wealth or that they get justice. However, that door is open for them if they choose to go through it, wherein the case of the African American, that door has been historically closed.

The Healing of the African American Soul

It is also of paramount importance that we understand that it was one reason we were subjected to the most inhuman treatment in the history of humankind. That reason being economics, all of the dysfunction, disenfranchisement, and every other disorder you can think of can be traced back to the economic motivation of the ruling elite. We must understand that this system, the total American societal framework, has been dead set against the economic establishment of the formerly enslaved people.

For this reason, we need to pay special heed to the work and leadership of people like Shawn Rochester. His work is focused on the concerns that address the peculiar needs of our people. It takes special people with the right sentiments, skills, and interests to deal with the unique financial needs of our people. The work that he and his family are doing through the Good Steward initiative is essential to change the financial health of our community.

This current work, The Healing of the African American Soul with Truth and Reconciliation, is a continuation of an ongoing effort to carry forth the mission of our honorable forebears. They pointed the way to the authentic human establishment of model community life. *Say: O People of the Scripture! Come to an agreement between us and you: that we shall worship none but The Creator, and that we shall ascribe no partner unto Him, and that none of us shall take others for lords beside The Creator. And if they turn away, then say: Bear witness that we are they who have surrendered (unto Him),* Quran 3:64. We are admonished to come to our common sense, decontaminate our social blood that keeps us from forming the clot of social intelligence to stop the bleeding of our wounded souls.

The Healing of the African American Soul

The un-natural language of black and white assigned to skin identification is a product of the true enemy of the human being. It is a concoction made to prevent the natural clotting of our social intelligence. Our continued use of these terms as labels for human identity takes us more profound in the bottomless pit of the spell. The truth is that it is hard to break habits that are so well established.

However, we must consider the cost, the inhuman atrocities perpetrated by so-called white people based on their false notion of a divine right of "white privilege." And yet and still, those that remain silent because of their meritless advantage receive the base of this false notion of "white privilege." While on the other end of the spectrum, we have wasted human capital, flushed down the drain of lack of human opportunity, and self-full filling prophecies.

The human being is created to be upright. From infancy, the struggle to stand up is clocked in our nature. We, as human beings, have been standing physically for a long time. Now is the time that we stand up morally and spiritually. We have a moral and spiritual mandate to be productive, using what we have to establish model community life. Building community means coming into unity.

Coming into unity means having a vision, a sense of mission, and purpose consistent with the design and pattern we are created on. Coming to unity then means also establishing a state of health. Health is described as a state of complete emotional and physical well-being. To arrive at this state, we must have a reckoning. We must confront the truth of our reality, the good, bad, and the ugly. We must establish a time for truth and reconciliation.

The Healing of the African American Soul

"Where justice is denied, where poverty is enforced, where ignorance prevails, and where any one class is made to feel that society is an organized conspiracy to oppress, rob and degrade them, neither persons nor property will be safe."
Frederick Douglass

Word Environment Exercise

The Word Environment Exercise was included in my last book and is included in this one because the content is also appropriate. It is unbelievably simple, yet many people are challenged by it. I created the exercise over twenty years ago. I came up with it as an idea to relate to my young nephew how we are programmed to see ourselves. Since that time, I have completed the exercise with many people, young and older, and it is quite revealing to see how people react to it. So, I would advise you to take the exercise now before you read any further.

I always give instructions as follows: There are two dots on the top of the form, one black and one white. There is a column of words in the center of the form with a line to the right and left of each word under the black and white dots. All you have to do is look at each word and make a checkmark on the right or left side of each word, according to how you relate to that word. There are no right or wrong answers. **Now, let's begin.**

The Healing of the African American Soul

	⬛ ___		⚪ ___
1	___	**Wrong**	___
2	___	**Clean**	___
3	___	**Right**	___
4	___	**G-d***	___
5	___	**Pure**	___
6	___	**Success**	___
7	___	**Death**	___
8	___	**Upright**	___
9	___	**Criminal**	___
10	___	**Winner**	___
11	___	**Down**	___
12	___	**Beautiful**	___
13	___	**Up**	___
14	___	**Ugly**	___
15	___	**Strong**	___
16	___	**Weak**	___
17	___	**Innocent**	___
18	___	**Failure**	___

The Healing of the African American Soul

19	____	Loser	____

Now that you have completed this part of the exercise go to part 2 on the next page and answer the last question.

Please, do it now!!!

____   **You**   ____

Please share in the space below the thoughts and feelings you experienced while completing this exercise. Remember that there are no right or wrong answers. Every participant has a different experience. What did you learn about yourself?

_____

_____

_____

_____

_____

The Healing of the African American Soul

The word environment exercise is a valuable tool that provides insights and demonstrates how people are programmed to see their world and, more importantly, how they see themselves in it. Armed with the knowledge of how our word environment is structured and how we are affected, we are in a stronger position to reconstruct our word environment consciously. Reconstructing our word environment equips us with the initial tools to remake ourselves and to remake our world.

Chapter 6: STAND UP

"Striving To Affirm Natural Development From a Universal Perspective"

The concept of STAND UP has been with me for a long time. My first thought centered on the need for us, as descendants of slaves, to raise the bar regarding our expectations of ourselves. I believe that our individual, family, and community life look just like the picture we have in our heads. I realized that in an environment where most of what we get, in terms of how we are presented in media and the word environment in general, is 99% negative.

To say that this overwhelming representation of negative imagery impacts how we see ourselves would be an understatement. How else do you think it could become a norm for men to walk around with their butt showing as a statement of being hip? How is it that our women, mothers, and to be mothers can come out in public with nearly no clothes on, with no shame? How can we take low-frequency words like bitches, mother f'- errs, hoes, niggers, and on and on and on and use them as accepted everyday language.

The point has been made that we have lost the moral high ground that we once stood on. That moral high ground were people who declared their lives as a statement to improve the lot of our people in all their actions and behavior. They called themselves race men and race women, and they lived lives worthy of emulation. I heard

The Healing of the African American Soul

the statement that the road to hell is paved with good intentions. I said at first that is not true, but upon further reflection, I thought that was true. In the English language, good can mean a preferred action over another option.

Many people are sick or dead because they choose what is good to them but not beneficial to them. As a people, we have lost the sense of what is beneficial to us as families and communities. Morality is undergirded by principles and beliefs that we live our lives in ways that our actions do not infringe upon the rights of others. It is also our moral obligation as individuals to work to benefit the life of the whole. Our American experiences have promoted indifference to these fundamental concepts of human decency.

We are not responsible for how we are treated or how others view us, but we are responsible for reacting or responding. A reaction is done without much thought and most certainly without any planning. A response, on the other hand, is with thought and some degree of planning. One of the main points in this book is that we have been conditioned and steered down a path of reaction to all the opposition we have faced to our efforts to establish ourselves on equal footing with others in society.

In every known case, where there were attempted responses to the systematic disenfranchisement of the formerly enslaved people, those efforts were met with violent opposition, either overtly or covertly. Therefore, the pictures we have in our heads are formed out of a reactionary worldview. The best way to see this is to understand that reactionaries are always fighting against something, not for something.

The Healing of the African American soul

Our culturalization under slave culture and its language system has not allowed us to have a realistic picture of productive family and community life. Proof of this is the fact that we do not have wholesome, productive community life. Natural family life and its extension, natural community life, cannot exist in a vacuum.

The community, which is the evolution of families coming together through mutual cooperation to meet their everyday needs, must have branches that stem from the trunk of the community's holistic needs. These needs fall under the domain of the social birds (social institutions) mentioned earlier. Where natural community life is established, these social institutions make up the framework or infrastructure for how the individuals and families' educational, economic, governmental, and cultural needs are addressed as they move through the cycle of life in an ever-evolving process of growth, maturity, decline, decay, and death.

All matter decline decays, and dies, and in the natural world, that process gives rise to a new life that grows and matures to produce and reproduce productive life. The formerly enslaved people were regulated to a 3/5's life in this respect. Slave culture designed our life to revolve around an incomplete life cycle; decline, decay, and death. Slave culture factored outgrowth and maturity, which is crucial in wound healing.

Therefore, our individual and family life has no framework or infrastructure to support productive community life. To have productive, natural community life, our ideas, concepts, thoughts, beliefs, and actions must flow on a complete cycle of growth, maturity, decline, decay, and death. They must decline or submit to the truth

The Healing of the African American Soul

of their own reality. They must decay or be broken down to expose the weaknesses and potential strengths in our human experiences. They must facilitate the death of our shortcomings while the strengths lie dormant, waiting for the nutrients to come and fuel our new growth and maturity.

Slave culture fractured our lives into a three-fifths worldview. Our senses to the degree that we do not see with our own eyes nor hear with our own ears. The oppressive word environment has conditioned us to see and hear the world through blackness or be-lacking-ness. As we have pointed out already, our diet was made a three-fifths diet, leading to the sad fact of our poor overall health condition.

But most important of all is this three-fifths word diet has led to this revolving cycle of decline, decay, and death. With such a world view, our lives revolve around how we feel, and we have been conditioned to think that material will make our lives better exclusively. So, we try to define our lives by trying to look better, not trying to be better. With all the material we have as a collective group, we could change our condition overnight if we decided to be better.

We will achieve it when we see wholesome, productive community life as new pictures in our heads (beliefs). First, I say again; we must decline or submit to the facts of our current reality. We do not understand the nature and impact of the words we use and how their low frequency keeps us walking around like a chicken looking down for crumbs on the ground. Next, we must allow for the process of decay. We must let the truth expose our

The Healing of the African American soul
weaknesses and potential strengths. As an example, black in nature is a beautiful thing that we cannot do without.

However, the black in our lives, created by slave culture, is not the black of nature. Black is the opposite of white, and it is a source of weakness that we are conditioned to deny. We are disempowered by language we do not understand, so we embrace a label that describes something physical as a reaction to another physical brand that is opposite. Our strength is not in our biological makeup; it is in our command over our physical makeup. The slave language will not allow us to gain that command.

Then we must die to our bad behavior and habitual way of living. When the physical defines us, the death we cause is the unwanted physical death of each other because we hate the black slave culture. We must die to the objectification perpetuated on the human being by the slave culture. We must let the nutrients in that dead matter give rise to new growth and maturity. The truth will set us free. The truth of our story is so rich and energizing that it will fuel our lives for many generations to come.

The point of STAND UP is to move away from the reactionary posture and toward a responsive posture that is true to our natural development. The title of this book should be Healing the African American Soul with Truth, Reconciliation, and Reparation. I stayed with the title without Reparation because of the overwhelming need for truth and reconciliation first. Knowing if this is done right, reparation is the only logical outcome. The case for reparation is made by many. Still, Shaw Rochester lays it out in unequivocal quantitative terms that the U.S. Government not only has a moral responsibility but, as a

The Healing of the African American Soul

matter of legal obligation, to provide a remedy to what it is principally responsible for.

The case is clearly made that our enslavement, that our emancipation with no means to be free, that the murder and the terror of violent mobs, that the sharecropper contracts, vagrancy laws, convict leasing, segregated housing, redlining, that we are over-policed and underserved, that we are the fuel for the prison industrial complex, that our poverty is a creation of government policy and total disentrancement of us, the formerly enslaved people, are direct or indirect actions of the U.S. Government.

There is no question whether or not the formerly enslaved people are owed reparation. The U.S. Government saw fit to pay the slave owners reparation at the end of the civil war for the loss of their human property. The Creator of justice will see to it that we get what we are owed. This we can be sure of. But we must do our part; our job is to STAND UP. Shaw Rochester was asked the question; does he support reparation.

He said yes and added that today if we got reparation, it would be a massive stimulus for the status quo because we do not have the infrastructure to manage an influx of money in a way that builds and retains wealth in our community. This realization is one of the main thrusts of STAND UP. We have to be proactive in our efforts to change our state from moving in a line of least resistance to all the challenges we face on a day-to-day basis. We must reorientate ourselves to STAND UP for what we declare is our right and duty as human beings.

Most recently, STAND UP as a concept has taken on new life from a paper I wrote and shared with some of my

The Healing of the African American soul

close companions. Much of the ideas and concepts expressed in the report were from writings that make up the content of this book. It was impressed upon me the need to take the views expressed in the paper to the next level, that being a call to action. A call to our individual and collective responsibility to STAND UP for what our forebearers prayed, fought, died, and lived for, our true liberation as human beings.

A small group of us begin to meet, exploring ways to frame our concerns in a movement that could attract others with a sense of urgency to address the vital issues we face as a community. From that group, we established an Ad Hoc committee. We chose the name for that committee to be CCEDG, Community Cooperative Economic Development Group.

The CCEDG is now a "C" corporation formed as an Ad Hoc group of African American citizens. We have united on mutual and common social concerns regarding the disastrous and challenging socio-economic conditions that we find ourselves subsisting in today, in America. This subsistence living under racism, oppression, police brutality, poverty, corrupt government is a most brutal form of continual deprivation and disenfranchisement for ourselves as individuals, our families, and our communities.

Against all human odds, the intestinal fortitude of our ancestors and generation after generation, coming from planned, institutionalized, systematic suppression, we are still here. Though it has proven to be a bitter pill to swallow day after day perpetually, we know we cannot stop now! We have a moral commitment under our Creator, a community commitment for our society, and an individual

The Healing of the African American Soul

obligation to our families to address and redress these morally imperative issues. We are consciously aware of these issues impacting our families daily, purposefully, in our American Shared Freedom Space.

We are working to make the most of what we have been blessed with and eliminate waste as an organization. We realize that it takes resources to accomplish anything as significant as what we must do. While at this point, our physical capital is limited, our human and intellectual capital is vast. And the more we unveil the truth of our story; the more abundant the opportunities for resources come to us.

We are working on multiple fronts to address the serious issues that face us in these trying times. Many people outside of our community are beginning to feel what we have been feeling. So, our situation is being compounded by a climate that is worsening for everyone. Therefore, we must ask ourselves, if we continue doing what are we doing today, where will we be a year from now, five years from now?

What I see is not a pretty picture if we continue down the path we are on now as a collective group. STAND UP is a game changer. It is a call to action, and it is a call to take responsibility, both individually and collectively. What follows is the STAND-UP document. What is to come is the campaign for the call for the Truth and Reconciliation Commission. The truth will set us free; the truth will set America free.

America must change her ways. There are holes in the ship of American society, massive holes of lies, and wicked ideas and concepts. America must face and own up to the truth; the cost for avoiding these truths is more than what

The Healing of the African American soul
we can comprehend. We have been forewarned of this day when everything done in the dark would come to light, and every tub must stand on its own bottom. This is the day of accountability.

Project Stand-Up

C.C.E.D.G.

Community Cooperative eConomiC Development Group

The Creator's Name, The Merciful Benefactor, The Merciful Redeemer

Prelude: Statement of Case

1. We, the people of the CCEDG, are a group of American citizens that have gathered as concerned members of the disenfranchised communities to preserve and advance the growth and development of the total human community. We have recognized the significance of the need for social, economic, and environmental development for all humans in our shared freedom space[1]. We have been impacted by this systemic global phenomenon, manifested in social realities heightened by the pandemic and prevailing economic conditions. We commit ourselves wholly to the remedial goals as the highest priority both now, into the twenty-first century, and beyond.

2. We acknowledge that the people of our communities have shown in many different ways an urgency and a need to address profound social problems, especially poverty, racism, unemployment, and mass incarceration, that affect the Formerly Enslaved African Descendants (FEAD) and social counterparts across the world. It is our task to address both the underlying and structural causes and the

distressing consequences in order to reduce social uncertainty and social insecurity in the life of humanity.

3.   We share the conviction that social justice, economic justice, and environmental development are indispensable. Prelude: Statement of Case for the achievement and maintenance of peace and security within and among ourselves, our families, and our global communities. Clearly, social, economic, and environmental justice cannot be attained in the absence of peace and security or respect for universal human rights and fundamental freedoms. These essentials are interdependent and fundamental to the establishment and sustainability of social order and the inherent intent written in the Articles of our U.S. Constitution.

4.   We are deeply convinced that the framework for our efforts to achieve a higher quality of life for all human beings is equitable social development that recognizes empowering the people through progressive education, eradicating poverty, and utilizing environmental resources sustainably as the necessary foundation.

5.   We acknowledge that human life is at the center of our concerns for sustainable development. And further, those human beings are entitled to a healthy and productive life in harmony with the environment.

6.   In the City of Atlanta, we gather here in a commission of faith, hope, love, commitment, and action. We will not succeed until we believe. And we will not believe until we love for our fellow human beings that which we love for ourselves. We gather with full awareness of the difficulty of the tasks that lie ahead but with a conviction that significant progress can be achieved, must be achieved, and will be achieved.

Project Stand-Up

7. The institutional reports of current conditions on all social fronts suggest that we are headed for some very trying times as a society. The experts state that we are in a posture to repeat the worst depression on record that we have faced since 1929.

Prelude: Statement of Case

8. Our foreknowledge concludes that because we are the products of the global institution of enslavement. As descendants of slaves, we are the most adversely affected by the state of health and the degenerating economic climates ever seen in history. Most importantly, we must know that these realities persist, not through happenstance; they exist to maintain the instituted lifestyle built on slave culture, which is designed for the total disenfranchisement of enslaved people in perpetuity.

Yes, the word is out. We are conscious that no one is coming to save us. While this is true, we know that we have been equipped with everything we need to save ourselves. The Time is Now! It is time to: STAND UP!

PROJECT STAND-UP!

DECLARATION OF COMMITMENT

SECTION 1 – VISION: Our vision is that of the establishment of model community life; where human beings, women, men, and children are grounded in their own reality; where the peace that Only The Creator Can Give us is the order of the day, where the power of the four social birds (Institutions) lift the members of the human community to ever higher standards in their relationship to The Creator and all of His creation. Each willing human being is encouraged and supported to pursue their unique purpose, talents, skills, and abilities as their G-d Given right to contribute to the growth and development of the greater human community. The worship of The One That Created us is demonstrated in our service to creation with conscious awareness of the crowned role, He Honored us with, as managers and custodians of His creation.

SECTION 2 – PURPOSE: The purpose of **PROJECT STANDUP!** is to serve as a foundational platform, where our ideas and concepts that have evolved through time can be structured in a way that bounds us in the undeniable truth of our own reality as fertile ground, thereby, commanding us to STAND-UP in constant pursuit of our noble aspirations and true human dignity, human excellence, and natural destiny.

SECTION 3– GOAL: Our goal is to free the captives, the human beings systematically deprived of their soul's right to life, liberty, and the pursuit of happiness.

SECTION 4– OBJECTIVES:
1. To enroll individuals and families in our vision for natural empowerment by advancing the work of thought leaders promoting good stewardship of what community resources we have. Our collective resources will be harnessed as a basis for building the economic infrastructure that we need for developing income streams for wealth generation and wealth preservation in our community.
2. To provide the education required for community engagement and active participation in programs and global business

opportunities that make the most of our resources and eliminate unnecessary waste. To advance strategies designed to increase family income by $5,000 a month within the first 6-months of enrollment and active participation in programs identified and vetted by our CCEDG team.

3. To consciously establish, grow and develop the four elevating social birds as a natural, balanced process of empowering our families and our communities. Further, these natural elevating processes are the framework for the infrastructure needed to generate and preserve the health and wealth in our historically deprived yet evolving communities.

Striving To Affirm Natural Development from a Universal Perspective

This is a call and an invitation to members of our human community to reclaim our lives as vanguards of our own fate. We live in a world where far too many human beings have very little intentionality or purpose in managing our lives. It is a fact that those who fail to plan, plan to fail. There is no group of people like us, the ex-slave community, where "planning" is so far removed from the essence of our ongoing reality. The nature of our slave experience and the residual effects of those experiences have conditioned us.

Consequently, that conditioning has made the role of "planning" as principal control agents and necessary directives in our lives almost impossible to visualize and undertake. A plan can be defined as a step-by-step, preconceived outline or a map to take you to a stated place, an actual location, or a specific destiny. The plan is activated based firmly upon where you are in the reality of your current situation.

To have a good plan that would take you to a well-defined place, location, or destination, one must first know where they are. That is, the point of origin must be acknowledged. To see where you are meant to be grounded in your own reality and conscious of your own situation and position in life. For one to not acknowledge the slave experience and its infective residual effects, as they were massively promoted historically in the ex-slave community, is an apparent denial of their true reality. This is arguably our number one problem today. How can one take the proper actions to resolve a particular issue if one never acknowledges that such a problem does, in fact,

Project Stand-Up

exist? Is the denial or unconsciousness of our own reality the primary reason we lead the world in all indicators of non-productive human community life? We certainly have enough intelligence!

To deny is a state of mind that refuses to admit the truth or the existence of what is, as it really and truly is. In other words, to "deny" is to buy into the lie. There is a law that says the mind, in its functional nature, cannot tolerate contradictions. So, when people buy into the lie, they must act according to it to validate the lie they have in the "eye" of the mind. This is why Steve Biko said: "the mind of the oppressed is the best tool of the oppressor." Why is this true? This is true because the mind is the mechanism, the agent that we use to process the words that we know, understand, and think with. Words are what shape and frame our perception of reality. To make and contain a slave, you must first create and define a *new* slave language encultured vocabulary.

Words make people, and the language of black and white is at the root of the slave language vocabulary that was used to produce the subsequent slave mind and social backwardness and flip flop culture. The unnatural meanings of black and white are encoded and embedded in the fabric of the society and in all of its structured social institutions by definition. In and of itself, the usage of the slave language makes it virtually impossible for the users of that language to see the true reality by its very design. It is a language built on lies, falsehood, and misrepresentation of nature's facts. It disregards the logical order manifested in nature and its reflective true, natural, scientific reality. The mind grafted by the oppressor can only go where the oppressor has planned and programmed for them to go, which is grafted in a model to serve the best interest of the oppressor.

Oppressed and vulnerable people are compromised and typically do not know where they really are or how they even got there; they usually do not understand what they have or what they need; subsequently, they do not know their strengths nor their weaknesses; and therefore, they do not know what to do. In short, they are not grounded conscientiously in their own reality. This is true, even with the so-called educated or perhaps the mis-educated ones from amongst us. Their values have become the instilled values of the imposing oppressor. They came to understand that the oppressor does not really value them, and therefore, inwardly, through a

Project Stand-Up

process of social transcendence, they do not truly value each other, even though each other is all that they truly have. The primary intent of the slave language is to keep the oppressed hypnotically asleep, unconscientious, and unaware of these factors that would undoubtedly change their state of being were they to become mentally conscious of these truthful, earth-shaking, moving, and fruitful facts.

Dr. King said, "If you don't stand for something, you will fall for anything." The language-defined and distorted nature of the oppressed mind falls for any and every trick that the oppressor plays or orchestrates on them, as devised, to either keep them down or send them plummeting backward.

However, we are now in a new day. It is time to STAND – UP! Imam W. Deen Mohammed, one of African Americas' most profound thought-leaders, said, "We need organization to protect the truth." Since the truth will set us free, we need organization to safeguard the truth that we know will set us free. One great truth we are given in scripture is that "human oppression is worse than slaughter." The most extensive oppression we have today is the word environment that denies us and will not enable us to accept our own reality. Project STAND – UP! Is a call for us to be grounded in our own reality. We must first be conscious of where we are and then conscientiously determine the destiny of where we want to go.

We must first be aware that the world we live in is a false social construct, fabricated on the slave language of black and white. This conjecture is not a language nor a sustainable pattern or supported by any aspect of nature. Even though the so-called white has more social advantages now than the so-called black, in the final analysis, and in the long run, there are no real, true winners in such a false social construct. As members of the ex-slave community, our greatest challenge is to rid ourselves of the encoded environmental meanings of black and white, as given in the slave language. The slave language makes it impossible for us as a people to love and respect each other honestly. So, we must socially reinvent ourselves with a definitive new language. With a clear contemporary language, we must simply redefine ourselves as natural human beings with the capacity and purpose to lovingly and sincerely pursue human excellence. That is, we must be reconnected to our natural abilities to be connected to the natural patterns that are related to creation. With our own reference line, we must establish the basis for seeing ourselves and our own true living reality.

We must know where we are. To understand where we are is also to know our strengths and our weaknesses. Our strength is that we have common shared experiences that bond us in unifying ways that we have yet to realize and utilize because of our shortcomings. In other words, our strength is *potential energy and productivity* that, if we harness, would make us diversified leaders in the world of humanity. Our shared experiences have earned us the right to demonstrate a cultivated, unique human spirit and a remarkable demonstration of human excellence in ways that are out of the reach of most people who have not experienced what we have endured over generations. We are like a new people on the earth! But our weaknesses, on the other hand, are rooted in our inability to recognize our own refusal to accept and embrace the truth in and of our own reality.

Striving To Affirm Natural Development from a Universal Perspective is envisioned as a tool to utilize that could provide the human (spiritual), social, intellectual, and material capital that would give us the strength to STAND – UP! as natural human beings. In revealed scripture, the Creator shows us that we must be arranged and organized in ranks to protect ourselves from evil. In nature, too, The Creator shows us the same principle: having power is having organization. We must STAND – UP! and organize, rooted in our own reality. We do solemnly believe that we have a core group of like-minded brothers and sisters that can set natural standards and remake the whole world and make the world whole. It has been stated by one of our foremost thought-leaders that "we must order our priorities and then obey the logic." Our number one priority is first to know that we are standing as believers, with purpose and vision for our lives, as the Creator intended it to be, for us. The logic tells us that we must arrange ourselves in ranks to sustain ourselves and to access the power and the strength that we have, in order to bring in the resources that we need, to establish the life that we want, that speaks to our human dignity and human aspirations.

Project Stand-Up

Logic tells us that we should establish our natural life on the principles of the four birds described in scripture -Education, Culture, Governance, and Economics'. Standing on the shoulders of our honorable ancestors, we pursue the development of the four social birds that will support us and allow us to soar above the gravitational pull of the ignorance inherent in the slave culture in this concocted, fabricated, currently established world domain. To provide the resources needed to give flight to all our social birds, we need wings to elevate us! We need a strategy that obeys the logic of our priorities. It is with this approach in mind that we propose the following:

1. That our Educational, social bird be the focus of our first effort for establishment, so that we may follow the right direction.
2. That our Economic, social bird be the next effort for establishment to properly orbit around our base essential needs while acknowledging that the logic in the other two complementary birds, "governance and culture," starting with our own selves, must also be inclusive for successful, balanced formation.
3. Logic also tells us that we must make the most of whatever we have and move forward while eliminating or mitigating any waste.
4. Logic further dictates that we must consciously make every effort to unify ourselves based upon our common social interest and aspirations.

WHEREAS we, the formerly enslaved people of America, endured nearly 300 years of physical bondage under a system legally sanctioned and enforced by the government of the United States of America: the abhorrent institution of chattel slavery,

WHEREAS this ungodly and cruel act against humanity was in violation of both the spirit and lawful position of the foundational Constitution of the United States of America,

WHEREAS the elite class of European Americans contrived and promoted through the weight of law, authority, munitions and their wealth status, the creation of "white" as an ethnic label out of fear, in order to divide and neutralize the intimidating power of the common masses,

Project Stand-Up

WHEREAS "whiteness" is a false social construct systematically interwoven into the fabric of every American institution, regulating the affairs of the American people, in a manner to deliberately disenfranchise the formerly enslaved and native people of America,

WHEREAS "whiteness" as a false social construct has given license to the United States Government and its designated privileged citizens to perpetrate unthinkable subhuman cruelty on their fellow human beings,

WHEREAS the United States Government and backed authorities took deliberate action to create the Jim Crow System, putting the formerly enslaved people in a social condition worse than they had been freed from,

WHEREAS the United States Government promoted and created segregation, even where it did not exist, as a matter of national policy, for the purpose of targeting support in areas that it falsely labeled as "white." While at the same time, withholding any and every manner of support to the formerly enslaved people, creating the ghettos and abject poverty throughout America,

WHEREAS we, the formerly enslaved people of The United States of America have been debased, blocked, heavily ladened and diverted at every turn, in our efforts and determination, in our unwavering mission for self-reliance and self-determination.

AND WHEREAS the prevailing wide gap in the wealth and the health disparities of our families are the direct result of proven facts establishing that we are and have been historically under served and over policed, impoverished and overly drugged by design; creating an overwhelming waste of human potential, too often confined by a legal system or in a prison industrial complex. We, the under-signed, affix our signatures in support of the establishment of a remediating, healing institution of justice "Truth and Reconciliation Commission."

Signature

Waliyyuddin A. Sabir

Daoud Shariff

Latifah Amanee Akram

Abdul Jaami Hakim Yamini

Angelene Permenter

Teresa Bell

Zafir A. Al Uqdah

Edward F. Jordan

Marcus M. Sabir

Yahya A.M.A. Hassan

The ideas and concepts in this Declaration of STANDUP are grounded in the content of this book. We believe that a strong case has been made on moral and spiritual grounds to call for a Truth and Reconciliation Commission. To move this initiative along, we seek one million signatures on this document toward establishing that commission. The following is an open letter that we are sending out seeking support for this effort.

Dear Human Family,

Many people have been on the front line of the fight to bring human dignity to the formerly enslaved people. We thank the Creator for them all. But there is no time like the present to do what life, justice, freedom, and equality demand of us. The lies, alternative facts, and plots to derail humanity from the path of its pursuits of human excellence are being exposed. Correcting wrongs so grave is a process and can be painful. However, pain is temporary and a necessary sensation in the healing process; it is a price worth paying to bring about a truly healthy state.

I have written a document, STAND UP a Declaration of Commitment, which is an acronym for Striving To Affirm Natural Development from a Universal Prospect. The content of this document is grounded in the text of my latest book, "The Healing of the African American Soul with Truth and Reconciliation." This document is the launch of a campaign to secure one million signatures supporting the establishment of a Truth and Reconciliation Commission.

Along with this open letter is the PROJECT STAND-UP Declaration of Commitment. Your support in this campaign is highly appreciated.

A servant for the upliftment of humanity.

Waliyyuddin A. Sabir

Also, as a part of this platform, we have identified some signature programs as a part of a portfolio of opportunities that we believe are necessary for achieving the objective laid out in this document. We realize that creating the resources we need to do this work is substantial. Our needs as individuals, families, and communities are likewise significant.

We have been functioning as President Johnson described, hobbled with chains around our legs for 400 years, brought up to the starting line, and told to compete. It is unrealistic for us to think that we can compete on such an unequal playing field. What we know is man plans, and the Creator plans, and He is the best to plan.

We now have systems that level the playing field. Cryptocurrency and blockchain developments are, in my belief, G-d sent if we use them right. These are decentralized systems created to protest against a corrupt government and business practices everywhere. We have in our portfolio programs that we believe will allow us to compete on equal footing. Those programs will be forthcoming in a suitable format for presentation.

On our website, we will go into greater detail on the programs and opportunities that we have vetted for your consideration to aid our economic empowerment. We are also open to ideas that anyone can share to help move the needle for our real growth and development.

In a recent conversation I had with Mr. Shaw Rochester author of the books "CPR for the Soul" and "Black Tax," h expressed that we are off the mark if we are not talking and working for true economic empowerment.

I pray that this work is a contribution in that direction. May the Creator of us all bless all of our good intentions, good works, and faithfulness to establish and maintain the human excellence in our DNA, Divine Natural Ability.

Thank you for reading this book; any shortcomings are mine, any benefit received from this work is by The Grace and Mercy of The Creator.

Social Science / Philosophical History

"America cannot be whole until the truth and nothing, but the truth is told."

> The mind cannot tolerate contradiction. The poor state of our mental health is undergirded by centuries of fiction. People cannot live in states of extremes. What appears on the surface is always more than what it seems. You cannot judge a book by its cover. You must dig inside to reveal and discover. Truth is our friend. It's the only thing standing in the end. *Wali Sabir*

WITHIN THESE PAGES IS A BALM FOR THE WOUNDED SOUL AND A STRATEGY FOR HEALING A BROKEN NATION.

You are the cause in the matter and this book demonstrates...

- The true adversary of the human being

- The plan to objectify the entire human family

- The proliferation of the real (WMD) Weapons of Mass Destruction

- The true meaning of three-fifths of a human being

- The healing frequency of truth

- The cascade of social healing

- The elevation of society to civilization on the wings of four social birds

- The creation of slave culture through the fabrication of a slave language system
- The human skin is not responsible for the atrocities committed in its name
- The creation of both "black" and "white" are social constructs to subjugate and dominate people.
- The reactionary nature of "black" embedded in the slave language system.

Afterword

Wali Abdul Sabir has been and still is engaged on multiple fronts. He is a prolific writer of both prose and spoken words and a master carpenter, par excellence, and a community organizer. Leading up to this latest book, Wali Abdul Sabir has written three previous works that I urge all adults, particularly parents of the youth, to both read and utilize as an insightful guide and a road map. As a collective, they have been written to help us strategize, navigate and assist us to effectively plan our honorable future on this planet earth as a body of progressively engaged human beings.

His other three books in this series are: * "The Reconstruction of the African American Male" * "The Anatomy of Change," and * "Liberating Minds from an Oppressive Word Environment." Order your copy today!

Oh, my people of the planet earth, who incline toward your own original human nature, do not despair! The forces of heaven and earth are committed to completing this purification and rebalancing natural processes. Come what may hold on to your original human nature, which is to be Moral, Ethical, Noble, and Upright. Ameen.

By ABDUL-JAAMI HAKIM YAMINI

Made in the USA
Columbia, SC
14 January 2022